MAN AND LAND

MAN AND LAND

in the

UNITED STATES

By

MARION CLAWSON

UNIVERSITY OF NEBRASKA PRESS

LINCOLN · 1964

Publishers on the Plains

UNP

MANUFACTURED IN THE UNITED STATES OF AMERICA

Contents

List of Illustrations

ILLUSTRATION CREDITS

Acknowledgment is given to the following sources that have provided illustrative material used in this book: Drawn especially for this book by Federal Graphics—Figures 1–8, 10, 14, 18, and 20. Provided by the Bureau of Land Management, Department of the Interior—Figures 9 and 11. Used by permission of Dodd, Mead & Co. from *Uncle Sam's Acres* (1951)—Figures 12, 13, 15, and 16. Used by permission of Johns Hopkins Press from *The Federal Lands: Their Use and Management* (1957)—Figure 19; and from *Land for the Future* (1960)—Figure 31. Used by permission of Rand McNally & Co. from *Land for Americans* (1963)—Figures 24, 26, 27, 29, and 31.

CHAPTER 1

What This Book Is About

Through the long ages of history and prehistory, man has been dependent upon land and its products for his food, fiber, fuel, and shelter. In his earliest days, he gathered seeds and nuts and hunted wild animals. Later he began to practice simple crop growing, and he domesticated animals. As the centuries went by, his ability to wring from the earth what he wanted for his comfort grew. He mined minerals, including the fossil fuels such as coal and oil, and his agriculture improved. He began to use the forest for more than a place to hunt—he discovered the value of lumber and of pulp to produce paper. Today, at least in our country, we have a complex industry, a high standard of living, and a rich total culture. To those living in cities, it may seem as if our dependence upon the land had decreased. In one sense it has, for we are less the prisoners of the natural conditions our forefathers found; but in another and deeper sense we are as dependent upon the land as ever, for its products and services are basic to our whole way of life. With all our great scientific and technological progress, we still depend upon the soil for our food and upon the forests for important building and service materials. Moreover, we have come to value the outdoors more for the rest and recreation it gives us—rest and recreation which a poorer nation could not afford to enjoy.

Part of man's relation with land has been and is technological—knowing how to use the many and varied properties of the land to his ultimate enjoyment, comfort, and security. This aspect of the man-land relation is highly important; being tangible and dramatic, it has often been discussed by many writers.

There is another relation of man to land, however, which shall be the focus of our book: under what social arrangements, laws, and customs has man been allowed to use the land, and how has he in fact used it. This is more properly a man-man relationship than it is a man-land one. Men, acting through the tribe, or the family, or the government, have set up rules under which other men are allowed to own, sell, buy, lease, inherit, and otherwise use land for their benefit. Sometimes these arrangements are specific and written, perhaps highly complex and detailed; sometimes they are less definite, subject to interpretation by the stronger for their own ends. In their totality, these various arrangements constitute a system of land tenure for that time and place.

The way men in any time and place use land (including all its natural qualities, such as forests) depends in part upon their technological skills and abilities, and in part upon the man-man relationships they have created or tolerated. Both are important; sometimes one seems more important than the other, but neither is ever wholly missing. Our concern in this book is chiefly with the way in which man has used land in the United States, under laws and conditions established by other men. We shall be concerned with land history, and how the various arrangements came into being and how they operated. But we cannot ignore technology, for it has often affected how the laws and customs worked out in practice.

INFLUENCE OF PHILOSOPHICAL IDEALS

The kind of land tenure system (laws and customs) that people create and use depends in part upon their natural environment. In an arid climate, for instance, they are likely to have different laws relating to use of water than they will have in a humid climate. But usually the basic philosophy of a people affects its land tenure and its land use even more than does the natural environment. In this country, for instance, we believe that every man should have the right to bequeath his land as he chooses, and that children of a man who dies without a will have a right to his property, often an equal right for each. In many countries and in many times, it was not thus; a man was limited severely in the way he could bequeath his property. Perhaps the eldest son received it all. In the United States, by and large, titles to land are clear and enforceable in the courts; the poor and the weak have their rights protected as well as the rich and the strong. It has not always been thus in the world, and it is not thus in many countries today. Above all, we believe in private property in land; in the Communist countries of the world, private property in land is absent or severely restricted.

We shall not try, here or later, to set forth in detail the American philosophical ideals. This book is aimed at an American audience, and most Americans are reasonably well familiar with our total national philosophy and culture. In the chapters which follow, we shall try to show how the American philosophy, as far as it relates to land, evolved and changed from earliest colonial times to the present. While much of our philosophy about land has remained relatively constant, there have been some changes; and in particular there have been changes in the way certain philosophies have worked out in practice.

AMERICAN LAND HISTORY IS DRAMATIC

American land history is dramatic, at least to this author. Small bands of colonists landed on a strange coast, and managed to survive and increase, in spite of great hardships

3

and many setbacks. They were determined to establish a society in which the common man had larger rights and a better life than in the countries they had left; but often there was divergence and even conflict within their ranks as to these aims, and more as to how to achieve them. The exploration and settlement of the continent is one of the most exciting parts of our history—trappers, traders, frontiersmen, cattlemen, homesteaders, miners, and many others cross the pages of history. Everywhere it was land which drew them on, which held them in hospitable spots, and which engaged their greatest energies and deepest interests.

The Revolution, the acquisition of the Louisiana Purchase, the other great territorial additions, the disposal of the new public lands to settlers—and to speculators—are all colorful parts of our history. Later, the rise of a system of permanent public land ownership, with our great national parks and national forests, form a unique episode in world land history. The rise of our wondrously productive agriculture, the transformation of the nation from an agricultural to an urban one, as the great cities grew and grew— all this is a more recent part of our land history. The great forests, once deemed boundless and often destroyed as a liability, have come in very recent years into new productivity. All of these, and many other, facets of land history present dramatic episodes and colorful tales.

One reason why land history is dramatic is that it is human history. Though we refer to land use changes, in every case there were flesh and blood people behind the changes —noble people, selfish ones, brave, timid, great, and ordinary, in the proportions those qualities usually are mixed in a nation or large group of people. We cannot dwell on the colorful human episodes of this long land history; our focus must be on the large changes, in the mass effects, but the reader must not forget the men behind the statistics and the laws.

4

It is our hope that we may communicate some of this drama to you, the reader. We think the tale worth telling for its own sake alone. But, more importantly, we believe no one can truly understand the United States today who does not know at least the major parts of our land history. Too often, that history is presented in the form of laws passed, of political battles fought and won and lost. These are indeed important, but the most important of all are the actions of the mass of people. The rush to settle the "West" —a west which started with Ohio and ended with California —and the rush today into the great outdoors, owned by the federal and state governments and managed by their bureaus, are fully as significant as any laws. At the base of our whole economy and culture is private ownership of property, including land; and that in turn traces back to the history of the land.

LAND IS STILL IMPORTANT

More than two thirds of our people now live in cities. They buy their food at a supermarket, buy or rent a house or an apartment from a builder or landlord, buy clothing at a large department store, and travel over land covered with asphalt or cement as they drive to and from work. Moreover, they read in the newspaper of new plastics and synthetics made from common raw materials such as salt, air, and coal. What a far cry from their ancestors of a century or two ago, who grew nearly all their own food and whose diets were limited to what they grew; who kept sheep to produce their own wool, which they carded, spun, and wove into cloth from which clothing was made; who cured hides from the animals they slaughtered, to make the shoes they needed; who cut from their own woods the logs from which houses and furniture were made, and which provided the fuel to heat—more or less—their houses. All of this was typical one hundred and fifty years ago; some of it, people can remember who are no older than this author. How many people have ever churned butter from milk they extracted from the family cow?

Contemplating these enormous changes in typical modes of living, one at first is tempted to say that man today in the United States is less dependent upon the land than were his ancestors. The dependence is less direct and less immediate, truly. Today we buy and consume foods produced in nearly all parts of our great nation—and from other countries as well. Ample stocks of all storable agricultural commodities have erased the fear of famine or shortage from our collective mind. Many hands, in many places, and much complex machinery intervene between the cotton field and the pretty dress in the fashionable store. But in a more direct sense we are as dependent upon the land as we have ever been. We still produce our food and fiber from the land; we still live and travel on it, and in fact we cannot avoid our full dependence upon it. In our cities we use small plots that we own or rent, that are ours to manage as we choose as long as we abide by general laws and rules; but we use to a large extent public areas, in the form of streets, parks, schools, and public buildings. Moreover, we work and shop in areas owned by others, whose services we buy or rent. In terms of acres, the land a typical city dweller uses directly today is small compared to the area his great-grandfather farmed; yet the intensity of its use is very high. It is incomprehensible that we will not always be dependent upon land, in a changing but nevertheless highly important way.

CHAPTER 2

What the Early Colonists Left Behind Them

In order to understand land history in the United States, one must know what the early colonists left behind them when they came to the New World. The kind of world they had known, and even more the kind of world they wanted for themselves and their children, conditioned their aspirations, their ideals, and their outlook. And this in turn greatly affected the way they used land in what is now the United States, and above all it affected how they permitted their fellow men to own, lease, bequeath, and use land.

Colonists came to the area now included in the United States from several countries of northern Europe—France, Germany, Holland, Sweden, Spain, and others. In this chapter, however, we shall consider the role only of the colonists from England. There are several reasons to justify this emphasis upon British colonists. In the first place, they were a substantial proportion of all early colonists to the United States. Second, the colonies that ultimately united to form the United States were ruled by England for a comparatively long period of time. And, last, British ideas on land use, land ownership, and land tenure gradually came to prevail and to dominate the colonial experience, and from this the later national experience. Other colonists left their traces upon land use and tenure, as for instance the Dutch in New York State, where lordly estates of patroons continued for many decades. One other relatively large influence was that of the Spanish, who came up by way of Mexico into our Southwest. But for our purpose, we can ignore these interesting variations on the general pattern. The reader should simply be aware that differences did exist.

FEUDALISM

When colonists from England first began to come to the United States, in the early seventeenth century, feudalism was already beginning to break up at home, though its traces were long to be seen.

Feudalism has a long history. Some aspects of it reach back to Roman times. It was developed into a major institutional force by the Franks and in Germany; Charles Martel and Charlemagne found it a useful tool for governing in their troubled times. It developed somewhat independently in England, although the Saxons had brought it from Germany. With the Norman conquest of England after 1066, feudalism in the Frank fashion was imposed strongly upon England.

Throughout its long history, feudalism has had two major components: a system of personal relationships, and a form of land use and land tenure. It arose or was extended in troubled times, when some men placed themselves in the service of other, stronger, men for protection. A system of personal service and loyalty arose, with obligations from the vassal to the lord, and from the lord to the vassal. Given the lack of competent general government, especially through the long Middle Ages, feudalism surely offered great advantages to all parties. But it was also a system of land tenure.

Small landowners, often fearing they might be forcefully displaced from their lands, would give their land to a powerful lord, in return for a tenancy right for themselves, possibly for their children also, on the same land. Lords with political and military strength found other ways of adding to their estates. In the absence of well-developed markets for agricultural produce and in the absence of a money economy generally, a form of tenure under which the tiller

FIG. 1.—FEUDALISM

Under feudalism, the men who worked the land were forced to comply with the lord's rules; all had to farm and live in a pattern dictated by custom. Income was low and living conditions poor, and there was little hope for a better future.

of the soil paid the landlord in produce and in labor was a natural development. The vassals were given fiefs, or rights to land (as well as other kinds of rights). Sometimes these rights were hereditary, sometimes not. The rights were often hedged about with restrictions, as was the use of the land itself.

Feudalism vitally affected the kind of use that could be made of the land. A vassal (or tenant, in modern language)

9

would usually have several parcels of land in different locations; after using them a few years, the land would often be divided differently among the vassals. This was done to prevent one man from getting all the best land. But the kinds of crops and the rotation was often prescribed by custom or by the lord. One big area would be for winter grain, another for summer grain, and a third fallow, for instance; and each vassal with a plot in each area had to follow the same crop practices as his neighbors. After harvest, the fields were often opened to grazing in common. There were in addition often meadow and pasture lands used in common. This system had its logical history, but it nearly always persisted long after its usefulness had ended, and in the end it became a serious impediment to experimentation, change, and progress. In the end, in England the Enclosure movement ended the common land and led to a different use of crop lands as well as greatly changing the role of the vassals or tenants.

Although we have generalized about feudalism, actually it had many variations, even within England, and still more when the countries of the Continent are included. A major characteristic of it everywhere was a lack of definiteness, of flexibility to meet political pressures and military strength, of ability to change with changing times. Much of it was a matter of custom rather than of law, although as time went on the terms of the feudal structure increasingly came to be spelled out in written law.

One can also generalize about feudalism to say that under it the mass of people lived poorly, with limited and somewhat uncertain legal and political rights, and with little opportunity for improvement. To these people, on the land and tied to it but with limited rights in the land, ownership of land loomed as the most desired of all states, the best of all opportunities for security and income. With this direct background, or indirectly through parents and grand-

10

parents, people were greatly excited about the prospects of migrating to a new land where they could own land.

LAND USE AND TENURE CHANGES UNDER WAY

Feudalism changed throughout its history, but the rate of change accelerated after the middle of the fourteenth century. The rise of national governments, with at least some power to maintain law and order and to govern generally, tended to weaken the need for the personal aspect of feudalism. Over the decades and centuries, the terms of the feudal land tenure arrangement changed slowly, and in the end to a major degree. The terms of the land tenure became more and more definite; service and other obligations tended to become converted into cash obligations, and these to diminish relative to the income possibilities of the land. When the Black Death swept England in the mid-fourteenth century, it killed between 30 and 50 per cent of the whole population, and apparently a higher proportion in the rural areas. Lords found themselves without manpower to farm and sustain their estates; landless men of different classes were able to, and did, demand better tenure terms. This calamity thus gave a major impetus to the social changes slowly under way, and it advanced by many years the slow evolutionary process whereby vassals were gaining more control over the lands they tilled.

As feudalism changed, it gradually emerged into the manorial system, with lords, tenant farmers, and laborers, which characterized England for later centuries, and which still persists to a degree. One cannot put a date at which feudalism disappeared; many features were severely altered by the Statute of Tenures in 1660, but a few vestiges remained as late as 1922. Gradually, the rights of the lord to the land began to resemble private land ownership as we

11

know it today, and the rights of the tenant came to resemble those common today. In part, this was an evolutionary intellectual process, with new concepts of property, of rights, and of obligations evolving. But in large part it was also a long slow struggle of the underprivileged for freedom, economic opportunity, and a better life—all of which they saw in terms of land and their rights to it. In this latter respect, the changes in England from perhaps the thirteenth to the nineteenth centuries were not unlike those going on today, at a faster rate, in many underdeveloped countries of Latin America, Asia, Africa, India, the Far East and the Near East.

Another factor which affected the changes in feudalism was the rise of the towns and cities. Although England was still a rural country by modern standards well into the eighteenth century, yet from the time of the Black Death onwards significant numbers of rural people, often those with the least foothold on the land, migrated to the cities. A rise of manufacturing and of trade provided them with employment. This outlet, while it affected only a minority of all the rural people, nevertheless had its effect upon land tenure also. In this respect, the underdeveloped countries today are similar since they too are experiencing urbanization.

LIVING CONDITIONS IN
COLONIAL TIMES

When colonization of what is now the United States started, back in the early 1600's, living conditions for everyone everywhere in the world were miserable by modern standards. Medical standards were primitive; half or more of the babies born died in the first year, and life expectancy at birth was probably less than thirty years. There was no conception whatever of the modern germ theory of disease, and hence no steps were taken for sanitation. Even as late as 1800, when George Washington was dying from pneumonia, the doctors bled him rather than nursed him. Food was miserable, often inadequate in amount, certainly lacking in variety and taste for the poor man, and without any regard for modern concepts of nutrition. Shelters for the poor were mere hovels, small, cramped, dirty, dark, little more than man-made caves. Even the lords lived in drafty castles, cold in winter, totally lacking in what we regard as the basic necessities. Electricity was, of course, unknown and undreamed of; light was supplied by torches or candles, but all of the many modern conveniences we know, operated by electricity, were absent. So was modern plumbing. Someone has said of the eighteenth century: it stank. People went unwashed for months at a time. The rich used perfumes to cover up body odors and spices to conceal the flavor of rotting meat; the poor lacked both.

Moreover, for a substantial proportion of the people— the poorest—mere existence was a problem. Food was often barely enough to sustain life, and sometimes not that. While the Black Death (the plague) was spectacular even for those days, illnesses such as smallpox were common and usually fatal. The position of the relatively rich was better, yet poor by our standards. Someone has said that King John never enjoyed the comforts that John King, an ordinary citizen, enjoys today.

Perhaps of equal, or possibly of greater, significance was the fact that there was little hope for anything better, especially for the lower-income people. Society was highly stratified socially, politically, and economically. In an earlier period vassals were tied to the land, not free to go when and where they liked. Later, although free to go, there may have been no better opportunity anywhere. Political rights such as suffrage were limited to a small minority and often were restricted to those who owned land. A man was likely to find himself confined to the same life his father had led, with little prospect that his son could do better.

When colonization of North America began, the hardships of travel across the Atlantic and of settlement in the wilderness were very great, and there was real danger of loss of life. Yet these hardships and risks must be contrasted

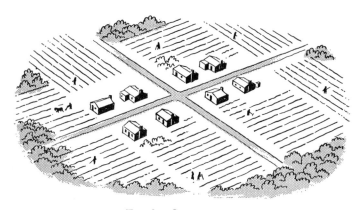

Fig. 2.—COLONIALISM

In the new colonies, life was hard. Often there was not food enough, modern comforts of life were wholly lacking, and many took sick and died. Yet each man on his own farm represented a degree of independence and a hope for the future never before known.

with living conditions in England and other European countries at the time; the gap between the frontier and the home country was vastly less than it would be today. Life was hard where they were, and hope was lacking; and a rough life but with hope for land and independence seemed attractive to many.

THE NEW WORLD, A BEACON OF HOPE

We today cannot easily imagine the immense, intense popular interest in the New World back in those colonizing days. If we today should suddenly find a way to reach Mars, and if we should find there a congenial environment for life (which scientists say we shall not), the excitement that would ensue might resemble that of England and western Europe in the seventeenth century. Comparatively few people actually migrated; many others longed to do so but could not find the means or the backers; and others were excited about the new country but were unwilling to leave a familiar environment.

The early English colonists in North America sought many things there. Their desire for religious freedom is often stressed, and it surely was a real factor. Some wanted religious freedom only for themselves, being willing to suppress others who differed with them, even as they had been suppressed at home. Many sought economic and political opportunity—the chance for a higher income and for more nearly equal political rights. For the latter, land was certainly a major attraction. It was the ideas, ideals, and hopes that these people brought to the New World which influenced its land history so markedly.

CHAPTER 3

What the Early Colonists Found in the New Land

The new colonists to North America found a strange and primitive land, different from what they had known at home, and difficult to adjust to.

Forests were everywhere. With few exceptions, the eastern half of the United States was originally forested. The primeval forests were magnificent—huge trees, large, straight, and tall, with many more species than are naturally found in Europe. The forests stretched endlessly; an explorer could go through them for days, with no substantial clearings and no apparent end. The term "endless" came increasingly to be applied to the forests of the United States, and to remain as a description long after the end of the old-growth commercial forests was in fact in sight.

To the new settlers, these forests were both a blessing and a menace. They provided ready building materials and material for furniture and many needed articles. They provided fuel for heating, at first readily at hand, later somewhat farther away as the nearer forests were cut. Still later, the colonists, especially in New England, were able to sell the larger trees for masts for sailing vessels of the day, especially for British warships. In that day, a ready supply of good masts was almost as essential for military power as is ready access to a supply of uranium for nuclear weapons today. In these ways, the forests were an asset to the early settlers.

But the forests had other characteristics which created serious problems for the early colonists. The land had to be cleared of trees before it could be farmed. The huge trees had equally huge stumps, that could be removed only with the greatest difficulty, since the colonists lacked anything but the simplest tools. Many settlers were forced to girdle trees, letting them die naturally, and farming among the dead trees; or to remove the trees, leaving the stumps, and farming among the latter until they rotted and could be removed readily. Clearing a few acres was often the work of years, yet some cleared land to grow crops was necessary for survival. As trouble with Indians grew almost everywhere, the forests came to be dreaded as the harboring place for the Indians who swooped down upon the little settlements.

The popular attitude toward forests gradually came to be one of tolerance, taking their values for granted and assuming their extent and future availability as indefinite, and one of dislike and even hatred. These attitudes, ingrained from early days, were to persist long after the situation that had called them into being had in fact changed greatly.

The early settlers of course found no roads anywhere, nor were decent roads built for many decades. The Indians had some trails for foot and horseback travel, but most movement of people and of goods had to be by water. Early settlement stayed close to the water, either the coast or the small streams which led inland. The ocean-going sailing ships of that day were very small by modern standards and could often penetrate up the larger rivers for considerable distances. They could go up the Chesapeake Bay and the Potomac River, for instance, and load tobacco right from the planter's small wharf. Travel within the colonies was either by horseback or by small boat along the rivers and coast. The lack of good transport facilities was serious, yet

17

much less so in that age of self-sufficiency than it would be today. Even in England in that day, transport was largely by water and was severely limited. It will be recalled that the earliest railroads came two hundred years after the earliest colonies.

The early colonists of course found no towns anywhere. Their earliest settlements tended to be in groups, called towns in those days, but so small we would hardly consider them towns today. People built their houses close together for protection and for sociability; they farmed the adjacent fields to grow the food they needed. Beyond the fields were the forests, from which fuel and building logs could be hauled. The early settlement which later became New York City farmed land in what is now downtown Manhattan, for instance.

INDIANS

All of North America was occupied, after a fashion, by Indians, whose home it was and who obtained their living from the land. The Indian culture at the time of the earliest white settlement varied greatly. Some Indians practiced agriculture, especially corn growing; some depended heavily upon fish as a source of food; others were primarily hunters; and many used these and other sources of food in varying proportions. Some were largely nomadic; others had more or less settled places of residence.

When the earliest colonists came, the Indians were at first greatly puzzled by them, and they were not sure just how to treat them. Sometimes they were friendly to the new white settlers, showing them how to grow corn, for instance; but often they were hostile, regarding them as intruders who would harm or destroy the native way of life. In the latter, the Indians were surely right, for white settlement did in time completely destroy the original Indian

18

culture. At the least, one can safely say that the whites and the Indians had greatly differing cultures; what was acceptable in one culture was often condemned in the other. Yet there was surely trade between them, from the beginning of settlement and even earlier with explorers. The Indians were eager to get iron pots, fish hooks, beads, cloth, and other articles the whites could offer in trade; later, fire-

FIG. 3.—EARLY COLONIAL SETTLEMENTS

The early colonists in their little ships found a strange land, almost solidly wooded, in which the first settlers clung to small clearings in which they had built their houses. Indians, sometimes friendly and sometimes not, lurked in the forest.

arms and whiskey came to be major articles of trade, in spite of the fact that the object of the firearms was often the white himself. The settlers were eager to obtain furs for their own use and for shipment back to the mother country, as well as food and other desired products. Parenthetically, we should note that the possession of firearms and the desire to obtain furs for trade enabled the Indian to put new pressure upon his natural environment, which in time came to have serious repercussions upon it.

Nowhere was the contrast in cultures sharper, and for our

purposes more critical, than in the attitude toward land. The Indian concept of land ownership was completely different from that of the whites; he did not understand them, nor did they understand his attitude. The Indian regarded land as something to be used and enjoyed, even to be defended against trespassers, but not to be owned exclusively by one person, nor ever to be bought and sold in the commercial sense. One's tribe might be driven from its ancestral hunting ground by war, but one still maintained sentimental attachments toward it and even claimed it as one's own. When the white man sought to buy land from Indians, the latter might agree, and accept a purchase price or gift, yet simply not understand what the white man meant. Later, when the white man sought to exclude the Indian from the land he had bought, trouble and conflicts arose. It was not simply that white men drove sharp bargains or that Indians reniged on bargains accepted, though there was some of each; more importantly, there never was a genuine meeting of minds, because each had such widely different ideas of the whole process than did the other.

To anticipate a little some of the discussion in later chapters, this divergence in concepts about land and the consequent struggle over land between white and Indian continued across the nation. Some whites sought peacefully to buy land from the Indians, yet the latter never really understood what was involved. Later, some colonies and the United States entered into treaties with Indian tribes over land, as though the latter were independent nations. That was an equally inappropriate way of dealing with the problem. Individual settlers persistently invaded Indian territory, in violation of treaties and agreements entered into between the United States government and the Indian tribes. Gradually we drove the various Indian tribes westward, forcing each displaced tribe onto tribes already resident in a region, leading to conflict among the Indians and between them and the whites. In the end, we drove the remaining Indians onto reservations, forcing them to adopt wholly new methods of living there or elsewhere. There was a fundamental incongruity between the Indians' method of living before the white man came and the presence of significant numbers of white men on the North American continent. If North America was to be settled and developed by white men into the kind of modern society it is today, the Indian's original mode of life was doomed. But this certainly does not endorse as wise or just all the actions taken by white men in their dealings with Indians.

LAND, PEOPLE, CAPITAL

The form of an economic society is influenced to a major degree by the relative proportions of land, labor, and capital. Today we have a large and well-trained working force and a rich supply of capital to apply to the land and natural resources of our country. The result is a rich and affluent society. When the early colonists came to North America, the situation was very different. Land was superabundant, people were very few in numbers, and capital of all forms was very scarce. The result was that both the economy and the attitude toward land reflected this situation.

Land in North America was claimed by various European countries—more precisely, usually by the king or crown in those countries. They fought over these lands, and reached treaties dividing up the land, wholly unconcerned with the fact that the Indians regarded it as theirs. The crown in turn conveyed land to settlers, but by different routes. For Massachusetts, Rhode Island, and Connecticut the crown gave grants of land to associations of settlers, who in turn parceled it out among their number in various ways. New York, after it was taken from the Dutch, and Virginia were considered as crown colonies, and rights to land generally derived from the crown, at least at first hand, although owners of land sold it to settlers. The other original colonies were generally of the proprietor type; a man or group was given a very extensive area of land—a whole modern state or more —which he both governed and disposed of to settlers, subject to some controls from the crown. Land was often given as a personal favor.

There was an effort, mostly unsuccessful by both the crown and the proprietors, to make land valuable, either when sold or when rented to settlers. The motive of financial gain was certainly high with some, lower with others; some had very extravagant and unwarranted expectations of gain; others were more realistic. In fact, however, land could not command a high price, either for sale or for rent; there was simply too much of it, and too few settlers. Settlers refused to pay purchase prices or rents, and nominal landowners were unable to collect them. In defense of the settlers, it must be pointed out (as we shall do in more detail in Chapter 4) that the cost of making a farm out of forest was high —high in real terms, of labor expended, if not of money invested; and the kind of farming possible in many areas did not provide much cash out of which to pay for land. With vast areas of land awaiting settlement and development, settlers saw no reason why they should pay high prices for any specific tract. Land did have value, it was highly prized and much sought after, and it was the subject of many transactions and much bargaining; but there was constant and major pressure to keep its money price low. Again, the attitudes toward the price of land, built up in the early colonial days, persisted through the whole era of land disposal, up to about 1920, and these attitudes have still left their mark, as we shall see in later chapters.

In the early settlements and throughout the colonial period, there was a great lack of workers to work the land. Many colonists obtained a piece of land of their own, farm-

ing it to produce their own food and other needed commodities, and selling little. Their standard of living was governed largely by the productivity of their land and of their
labor. Others sought to work land by the labor of other persons, and to produce export crops, notably tobacco. These
landowners sought workers in many ways. They brought
indentured servants from England, men who agreed to work
for a period of years (usually seven) without wages as a
means of repaying the cost of passage to the New World.
Various means were taken to encourage immigration.
Lastly, resort was had to slaves—men and women kid-
napped along the African coast and brought and made to
work against their will, with no hope of freedom. While
their numbers were small in the early colonial days, their
effect upon agriculture and upon society was considerable.

The productivity of most workers was low, by modern
standards. Most were engaged in agriculture or in simple
handicrafts; sometimes the same man did both, the farm
work in season and other work in the winter. There were
but few machines of any kind, and only simple hand tools
for all activities. Much of the land farmed at first was rather
low in fertility, and the settlers did not know how to improve it—and would have lacked the means to make modern
fertilizers even if they had known about them. As a result,
output per man—whether self-employed, indentured, or
slave—was relatively low. A living for one's self and family,
with some gradual improvement in living conditions, was
about the norm during the first few decades. Wages of hired
workers were relatively low. Thus the indentured servant
who received food and shelter but no wages was not so
much worse off than the free working man as one might
expect, if one thinks of modern wages.

It is probably impossible to say whether the early colonists were better off in the New World than they had been
or than they would have been in the Old; as far as we know,

no careful comparisons have ever been made. The flow of immigrants to the New World, while small in total numbers, was much larger than the return flow, indicating that more people thought they were better off in the New than in the Old World. Economic considerations certainly were not the

FIG. 4.—PIONEER FARMS WERE SELF-SUFFICIENT

The early pioneer farmer was almost entirely self-sufficient. He erected his own house and other buildings from trees cut in the forest; he grew his own food, made his own soap and leather, and wove cloth from wool, flax, or cotton for his clothes. He and his family worked hard and had a poor living by our modern standards. Yet this life was an improvement over earlier conditions under which his father and grandfather had lived, because it offered hope for a better life at some future date.

only ones; a better social and political position, more hope for the future, and—above all—land of one's own, or hope of getting it, were probably reasons crucial in importance to these settlers.

Capital, both as money and as productive goods, was scarce in the early colonial period. The costs of importation from England were high. Some articles for home, shop, and farm could be made by hand from local materials; plows were made of wood, for instance, and so was furniture. A few things were imported. Local manufacture gradually developed, yet until roughly the Revolutionary War, the colonies were deeply dependent upon the mother country for most of their capital goods.

GOLD, TOBACCO, AND EXPORTS

While the appeal of land for settlement was very strong, yet several promoters of colonies and many colonists hoped to get rich quickly. This attitude existed in the colonies along the Atlantic Coast; it had dominated the Spanish exploration and conquest of the lands further south; and it was to be a strong force leading to exploration and exploitation of the lands further west in the United States. Gold has always had a strong, almost mystical force to draw adventurers onward. The Spanish had struck it rich in Peru, where they robbed the natives of the accumulations of centuries. They conducted many fruitless searches elsewhere. English and other explorers and settlers along the Atlantic Coast sought gold, too. Fortunately for the development of the country, they found almost none.

Others wanted land to produce export crops out of which to make a fortune. Tobacco was the great success crop for this purpose. It was exported to England, and it paid for return cargoes of many kinds. Other crops, as indigo, were tried, especially in the South, sometimes meeting with limited success for periods of time. Much later, after the colonial period, cotton became the great export crop of the South. The desire to grow export crops fueled the efforts to import labor, including slaves, and was the basis for a plantation system of agriculture. So great was the emphasis upon export crops that the Virginia governor was forced in the early years to require a defined production of corn as a condition for growing tobacco, lest the settlers starve if boats with food from England were unduly delayed or went astray.

Farther north, agriculture took less the form of production for export and more the form of subsistence agriculture. New England exported fish and early developed handicrafts and small factories which produced their own needs and some export. Too, it earned its imports by a trading commerce based upon sailing ships of its own manufacture. In later colonial times it carried on a major trade in ship masts and other forest products, and in sugar and rum from islands in the Caribbean.

All of the economic activity of the new colonies, for the first one hundred years and more of their existence, was closely tied to the land. The bulk of the people lived on the land and practiced some agriculture, and the towns served primarily the people on the land. In the next chapter, we shall consider more explicitly how land was used in the colonial period.

CHAPTER 4

Land Use and Land Tenure in
the Colonial Period

The colonial period is almost half of American history; from the first permanent European settlement at Jamestown in 1607 until the Declaration of Independence in 1776 is nearly one hundred and seventy years; from the adoption of the Constitution in 1788 until today (1964) is little more than one hundred and seventy years. Half colony, half nation, is our history. For many reasons we tend to forget our long colonial status. It is true that our population then was small, its economy weak. But it was the events and attitudes of the colonial period which later dominated the nation, and which even today have important effects. The colonial period was an extremely formative one in American history. Big oaks from little acorns grow, but the oak seedling is small for many years.

The colonial influence has been felt in many aspects of American life. To take but one example, the early pioneer had to develop resourcefulness and independence. Usually there was no one upon whom he could lean. He had to fight his own battles and solve his own problems—and right tough battles and problems they often were. The frontier was no place for the weak, the timid, or the incompetent. Those frontiersmen who survived did indeed learn how to cope with their problems, acquiring an independence and a resourcefulness in the bargain which have had few equals in the world. These attitudes carried over into all phases of

27

economic, social, and political life; we prize them highly today. They tended to make the frontiersman "practical," often a little suspicious of theory and of ideas, and somewhat ingrown in his outlook upon life.

The colonial influence was nowhere more important than in the case of land matters. In this chapter we shall try to sketch briefly the outstanding characteristics of land use and land tenure in the colonial period; in later chapters, it should become evident to what extent this early experience was formative.

LAND SETTLEMENT PATTERNS

The way colonists settled upon the land depended upon several factors: their ideals about desirable ways in which to live, the relation between population numbers and land area (which we discussed in Chapter 3), and the political organization of the colony governments. Nearly all colonists were farmers, during at least part of their lives or part of each year, and the need to farm to make a living dominated the settlement patterns.

In the New England colonies, a group of settlers obtained permission, from the king in the first case and from the colony government later, to form a new settlement. Their requests were investigated as far as circumstances would permit—the suitability of the area for settlement and the competence of the group leadership in particular. After obtaining permission, the initial settlers moved as a group and established a new town. They surveyed the lands allotted to them and maintained title records on those lands. The village was laid out, often with a small common grazing and meeting ground in the center, with houses and big yards for gardens and buildings clustered around. Men worked together to clear the first fields, which were divided among all settlers; then later fields were cleared and divided similarly. In this way the settlement progressed as a whole, and each man had both good and poor land. As livestock were acquired, they were often herded in common, under the care of one man, on the uncleared lands of the village.

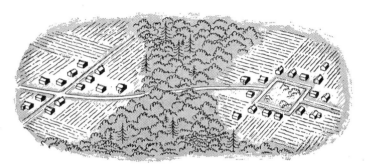

FIG. 5.—NEW ENGLAND SETTLEMENT PATTERNS

New England villages in colonial times were planned and developed as units. Houses were grouped along roads or around village greens, with fields stretching away from the village toward the forests. Lands were surveyed and land records kept.

Several good consequences flowed from this settlement pattern. Land titles were clear, land speculation was at a minimum, agricultural development of the whole village proceeded apace. Perhaps more important, the settlers learned to work together and to govern themselves efficiently and democratically. Settlements were typically of a single religious group, and religious intolerance was regrettably strong.

In the southern colonies, extensive use was made of the idea of headrights. As originally conceived, this system was not unlike the homestead law of more than two hundred years later. Each man who came to the new colonies was given, as a headright, a tract of land, usually 50 acres, on which he was expected to earn a living. Soon, however, men

29

who brought other men were given headrights. The ship captain, the planter who paid the fare, and the indentured servant each received a headright on the latter's entry into the colony. Still later, headrights were sold for cash, and were given fraudulently. Men who had headright land could

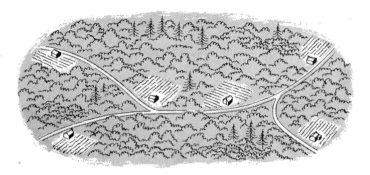

FIG. 6.—SOUTHERN SETTLEMENT PATTERNS

In the South, most colonial land settlement was an individual affair. Farms were scattered through the woods. Land surveys were often poor and land title records not clear. As a result, many small and irregular shaped pieces of land sometimes lay unclaimed between farms, and disputes over farm boundaries and land titles were common.

locate it where they chose, if the land was not claimed by someone else. Although they were supposed to have it surveyed and the deed recorded, in practice surveys were inaccurate and records poor. Numerous cases arose of two or more men each claiming the same piece of land; and disjointed small pieces of land between larger surveyed tracts were common. Speculation in land was very common; it was a typical way to acquire a fortune. Men settled their land, if at all, under arrangements individually made; each man tried to select the best possible land, leaving poorer land for others. Headrights formed one major basis for the

30

large plantations which gradually developed in the southern colonies.

In New England, the method of land colonization and the nature of the subsistence agriculture worked together to develop a system of rather small farms, each occupied and operated by its owner. Small farms also predominated in the middle colonies, in spite of some rather large land-holdings. Even in the southern colonies the small owner-operated farms greatly outnumbered the plantations, but the latter gave the dominant characteristics to the agriculture, the economy, the social life, and the political structure of these colonies.

The methods by which land was transferred from public to private ownership during the colonial period were many and varied. Title could pass directly from crown to landholder, but usually it went through the colonial government, whether proprietal or group settlement. The most common ways were those described above. But land was granted to men for military service, especially against the Indians; some land was sold directly for cash; and numerous other devices were used at one time or another.

AGRICULTURAL DEVELOPMENT

Although agriculture came in time to flourish in the colonies, at first it developed very slowly. Agriculture in England in the early seventeenth century was itself quite backward; the period of its growth and development came later. But the problems posed by the new country were serious. The crops the settlers brought from England were not well adapted to the new country; slowly, these people learned to grow crops native to North America, using methods developed by the Indians over long periods of time.

The earliest settlements often took advantage of open

lands, some of which may have been abandoned Indian cornfields. Soon, however, colonists were forced into clearing forest land. We have noted above how they killed trees by girdling and burning, farming among the dead trees and stumps while waiting for dead material to rot. Settlers often lacked tools to a degree unbelievable today. Often a farmer lacked such simple tools as spades, hoes, scythes, shovels, and the like. Plows were scarce during the early years, as were draft animals to pull them. In the new clearings, tree roots left in the soil would have made plowing nearly impossible for many years in any case. Settlers learned to dig small holes, with shovels or spades, and plant corn and some other crops in this way. Only much later, as fields were better cleared and plows were more common, were they able to grow wheat and other English crops which required widespread sowing.

The early colonists had particular difficulty with livestock. The long ocean voyage was expensive and livestock losses were high, so that animals in the colonies required more capital than many settlers had. The animals imported often died, especially in winter, partly because the colonists underestimated the severity of the winters and partly because they lacked good hay and other livestock feeds. It was several years before some of the earliest settlements acquired any horses or cattle, and many years before each farmer had his own. The settlements lacked good fences, and the Indians constantly sought to drive off or to kill the cattle for meat. Cattle and horses could be herded, but pigs presented a special problem. The pig can go semi-wild very quickly, foraging for itself but also destroying crops and gardens.

Gradually the settlers made agricultural progress in several directions. More land was cleared, and that already cleared was freed of stones, stumps, and roots. The settlers gradually acquired or constructed more tools and simple machines—crude indeed by modern standards, but enormously more productive than the earlier ones or than none at all. They learned better methods of growing crops of all kinds, and of harvesting and storing them. Livestock gradually multiplied in numbers and improved in quality. In New England, agriculture mostly continued to be of a largely subsistence character, the farmer producing what his family needed and largely consuming what the farm produced. He

Fig. 7.—Farm Tools in Colonial Times

The early colonists mostly had simple, even crude, hand tools. Oxen or horses for farm work were relatively very expensive, and many early farmers did not have them. The simple tools were often made of wood or iron, never of steel. The farmer's productivity with such tools was necessarily low.

earned cash to buy the things he needed by other activities, or he engaged in trade and barter. There were some exceptions; the Connecticut Valley became the first wheat belt of the North American colonies, for instance, selling its wheat in other areas. New England also gradually developed fishing, forest industries, and above all trade as major parts of its economic base.

Farther south, in the middle colonies and in the southern ones, agriculture was basic not only to the colonists' needs but also for export. Mention has been made of tobacco export; exports were roughly a million pounds annually twenty to thirty years after the first settlements began, but by the Revolution they had reached 100 million pounds annually. This was the basis of agriculture, trade, and gov-

FIG. 8.—FARM TOOLS NOW

The modern farmer has wonderfully built farm machines, almost always of steel. Tractors put many horsepower at his command. Large acreages can be plowed, seeded, or harvested in a day. As a result, gross output per man has increased manyfold.

ernment in Virginia, and later in Maryland. But other crops, such as indigo and rice, were important export crops at various times. Cotton was not an important crop until well after the Revolution. Repeated but unsuccessful attempts were made to grow hemp and flax and to manufacture silk.

TRADE

Trade was so important in the colonies, especially in New England, and its effects upon the whole economic life of the colonies was so great, that it requires a brief mention even in a discussion of land use and land tenure. It had, in fact, an important effect upon them also.

New England was not well adapted to agriculture, and in particular it did not produce any good export crop. On the other hand, it had excellent harbors, good nearby forests, and a working force that soon learned to build excellent sailing ships. Trade was carried on coastwise with the other colonies and with Europe, but the most notorious trade was a triangular one involving the West Indies and Africa. Molasses, sugar, and tobacco were brought home from the West Indies; rum was made of the molasses; rum was taken to Africa and traded for slaves; these were transported to the West Indies and sold there. Many an early New England fortune stems back to this trade.

The middle colonies developed exports of furs, wheat, and other commodities; their trading vessels and industry were not as extensive as those of New England. The southern colonies developed the tobacco, indigo, and other exports we have mentioned earlier; their trade with England was carried largely in English ships.

Trade of colonial products and by colonial traders was handicapped by numerous restrictive laws enforced by the English. Many products had to be shipped first to England, then later shipped to European continental markets, sometimes paying double duty in the process. Trade was severely handicapped also by a shortage of currency; resort to barter and to all manner of devices was necessary to overcome the lack of currency for ordinary transactions.

In spite of all these difficulties, trade to and from the colonies and by colonial traders increased and flourished. It was a major factor in their economy, and later it was the basis of naval power in the Revolution. Trade provided an outlet for surplus manpower and for capital and also provided a market for many agricultural commodities.

35

LAND TENURE IN THE COLONIES

During the colonial period, a great many important features of the later land tenure systems took shape and became more or less well established. The rights of government to regulate certain aspects of land tenure became firmly established. For instance, the right of government to tax lands, to take them for a public purpose upon payment of proper compensation, to enact laws regarding land fencing, hunting and fishing, and land inheritance was well established by the end of the colonial period. At the same time, the right of the landowner to sell to whom he wished gradually was established and was also well recognized by the end of the colonial period. The right to bequeath land as he chose was also established and recognized; when no will was left, laws gradually came to require equal or at least some inheritance among all children. This replaced the earlier English primogeniture, under which the oldest son took all the land and the other children received none. Various legal devices, known as entails, in England had enabled a landowner to assure that an estate would be kept intact and handed down to heirs of his choosing, even more than one generation later. These entails were gradually abolished in the colonies.

Most or all of the colonies had at first required quitrents of settlers. These were rents, payable in cash or in produce, which originally had been substituted for the labor a vassal had to perform on a feudal estate. Although these were supposed to be paid forever, by the terms of land grants to settlers, in fact the settlers persistently resisted paying them. As time went on, quitrents were reduced in amount or abolished entirely, sometimes only after long legislative struggles and extended delinquency on the part of the land users. Some quitrents still remained at the time of the Revo-

36

lution, but they were all abolished by the colonial legislatures during that period.

Land surveys and land titles, seriously inaccurate and deficient in the early settlement years in most colonies, gradually came to be improved. As land became more valuable, the need and importance for better land records was more evident. At the same time, as Indian unrest was pushed farther inland, it was easier to survey accurately than it had been earlier.

Comparatively little land was leased during the early colonial period, because the man who could undertake a lease could usually also undertake to buy land, which he preferred to do; yet some leasing did occur. As the land became more fully settled and as farming became more efficient, more and more landlords sought to lease their lands, and more and more tenants also wished to lease land. Tenancy thus became moderately common by the time of the Revolution.

Land tenures were highly variable during the colonial period, both as between colonies or districts, and as between different time periods. However, it is safe to generalize that the trend was toward giving the landowner greater rights to use his land as he saw fit, and toward reducing controls and restrictions over land use, whether the controls were from government or landlords. The idea of unrestricted land ownership, in sharp contrast to feudal land tenures, was widely held by the time of the Revolution, and it was to dominate American land history for a century or more afterward.

THE REVOLUTION AND LAND HISTORY

By the time of the Revolution, the colonies had reached a fairly high degree of economic development, for that era in human history. Their population was small—somewhat more than 3 million people, over 90 per cent of whom were farmers or closely tied to the land. Farms in the older districts were often quite productive and relatively prosperous; those along the frontier were less so. Of course one must realize something of the conditions of life everywhere in the world in those days. There was no electricity, hence no lights, radio, television, or any of the other host of modern conveniences dependent upon electricity; modern plumbing was still unknown; medicine was as primitive as we described it earlier for the England the colonists left; clothing and shoes were homemade, often coarse and poor; education was something only for the upper classes. While food, clothing, and shelter left much to be desired by our modern standards, yet in comparison with a few generations earlier they were good. The landowner had a large measure of security, legal and economic, and a large measure of independence. He had reasonable hope of bettering his material well-being as time went on. As we have noted, he was very much a self-sufficient, self-reliant character.

In the seacoast towns there was a small relatively wealthy class, mostly merchants, who lived in good houses, had fine furniture, drank imported wines, and otherwise enjoyed some of the luxuries of that day. Many had speculated in land, and nearly all depended in some degree upon trade with agricultural producers. The larger towns had newspapers, printing presses, and many other attributes of modern urban life.

The American Revolution was a social as well as a political revolution; it was the yeoman against the wealthy urban and landholding groups, as well as the colonists against the English; and it was the frontier against the coast, to some extent. We today often overlook that there was a considerable number of colonists loyal to the English king, who struggled against the colonists who wanted independence. There was an even larger group of colonists who largely stayed out of the struggle; agriculture and trade went on nearly as before in most of the colonies. The active revolutionists were clearly a minority. As we all know from our history books, the struggle was prolonged for seven years, and the colonists won in the end partly because they had the help of the French and partly because England was busy with European affairs, as well as because of the stubborn and skillful effort the revolting colonists made. With the winning of independence, those groups who had fought for it, and the ideals and attitudes they held, became more dominant in the national life.

Some specific consequences for land flowed rather immediately out of the victory. Tory estates were confiscated, subdivided, and sold to farmers, to help raise money to repay the costs of the war. Some, but by no means all, large landowners had been Tories, and subdivision of their estates meant a further strengthening of the landowning farmer. As we have noted, quitrents and certain restrictions on land inheritance were abolished, thus moving further in the direction of freedom in land ownership. During and after the war, grants of land were made to soldiers as a reward for their military service. In many cases, these soldiers sold their land rights, thus setting the stage for extensive land speculation and for the building of new large landholdings.

The indirect consequences of the Revolution, as far as land was concerned, were greater and more enduring. The whole pattern of public land ownership and disposal, and of private land ownership and use, which we shall describe in more detail in later chapters, grew naturally and more or less inevitably out of the attitudes toward land that had evolved during the colonial period and which were strengthened—one may almost say solidified—as a result of the Revolution.

CHAPTER 5

Exploration of a Continent

Exploration always preceded settlement and permanent colonization, in every part of the New World. The first explorers were looking for new lands to claim for their sovereign, or for booty, or for adventure, or maybe for all three. Sometimes they were looking for suitable sites for permanent settlement. Whatever their motives, the first visitors, who took back tales for the stay-at-homes, usually tarried but briefly.

Early European explorers had sailed along the Atlantic Coast, including up some of the navigable rivers; the names of Cabot and Hudson, among the English, rise to mind, and there were also the French, who sailed up the Saint Lawrence, explored the Great Lakes, and went down the Mississippi. These were the forerunners of the later permanent settlements of Europeans along the Atlantic Coast, which in turn evolved into the colonies and nation which we are today. These explorers carried back information and misinformation, and they fired imaginations for later settlement.

The Spanish had penetrated into the Southwest still earlier, but their effect upon American history, paradoxically, came later and was, on the whole, much less.

AFTER COLONIZATION

After the permanent colonies were established, exploration continued on an accelerating scale. The earliest explorations had been by water, and the difficulties of mounting a long expedition far from home base had always been somewhat of a limiting factor. Explorations after colonization continued by water, from a European or colonial base, and also by land. As soon as the colonies were firmly established, there was a good deal of informal and unofficial exploration of adjacent and distant lands, typically to the westward of the coastal settlements. Bands of men, intent upon trapping, fur trading, looking for likely future settlement locations, or just looking for adventure, traveled into new territory. Many of these explorations were never recorded for history; most were probably rather short, but some were certainly long both in miles and in time. Daniel Boone's adventures in Kentucky were of this general type; they have become legend, but there was solid fact behind them too.

Much later, especially after the new nation was formed, the official exploration mission became a much larger factor. The Louisiana Purchase stimulated great curiosity about the new territory; the Lewis and Clark expedition penetrated the northern Rocky Mountain area and through to the Pacific Coast. Later, Pike, Long, Fremont, and others led expeditions to or through the Rocky Mountains. These official expeditions typically resulted in more or less scientific reports of varying length and quality; though today these reports are museum pieces, at the time they exerted great influence. Such explorations continued well into the nineteenth century, past the Civil War; Powell, for instance, explored the Colorado River after that war.

There were also continued explorations along the Pacific Coast, after the permanent colonies had been established along the Atlantic Coast; but exploration and settlement of the two coastal areas proceeded independently until well after the Revolution. The Spanish and their descendants continued exploration and settlement in the Southwest and into California; the English explored along the Pacific Coast; and the Russians established permanent settlements in

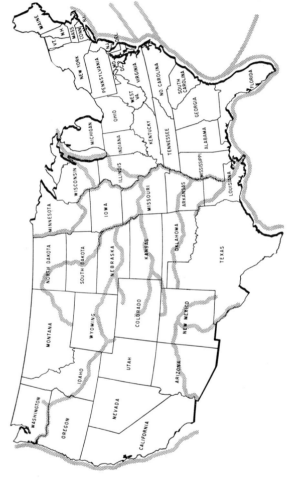

Fig. 9.—Early Exploration Routes

By 1700 the major coast lines and waterways had been explored, some several times, and a few notable land explorations had been carried out. In the next 150 years, major land explorations penetrated most of the West. On the scale of this map, we can show only some of the most common routes.

Alaska and as far down the coast as northern California. These explorations must have been romantic and exciting to have participated in; their accounts are often stirring, even when prosaically written. They were often genuinely valuable, both in providing more accurate information about poorly known regions and in exploding wild myths about them. Some of the expeditions were ill-fated with death, disaster, and failure; all involved hardship and danger. Although the prospect is tempting, we cannot attempt to describe them all, or even any one in detail; that would lead us too far away from our interest in the use man made of the land he found. We can only recognize that many explorations did take place, which in time pushed into every local area of the vast midcontinent which is now included in the United States. The permanent occupiers of the land benefited in numerous ways from the preceding explorations.

PEOPLE PRECEDED GOVERNMENT

Typically throughout the colonial and early national history, people preceded organized government in the lands along and beyond the frontier. There were always some frontiersmen who pushed onto land to which they had no right. That land might belong to other countries, or to Indians with whom treaties had not yet been concluded; or it might belong to their own government. These bold frontiersmen sometimes went in actual defiance of government, but more often without authority and without caring very much for the laws and strictures of a distant government.

This type of illegal entry was possible because some uses of undeveloped land did not require that its user have title to it, as far as the economics of the situation were concerned. That is, a trapper did not need to own the land

43

from which he caught fur-bearing animals. He wanted to range far and wide, and to move on when he wished. The same was true of the hunter, who lived much like an Indian. Some frontiersmen made lye, by leaching ashes produced by burning trees; the lye was basic to soap making in the settlements. These men had no desire to own land, as long as they could cut and burn the forests they found. Even

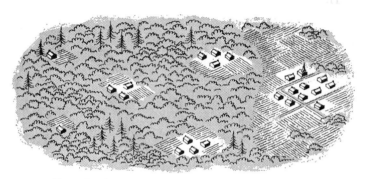

FIG. 10.—SETTLEMENT WAS THIN ON THE FRONTIER

As settlement in the United States generally proceeded from east to west, relatively fully settled rural areas gradually were replaced by more scattered settlements within forests. At any given date, some settlements had moved to the more remote frontier, leaving large areas of intervening lands undeveloped.

the primitive subsistence agriculture of the frontier could be carried out economically on land not owned by the occupier. His cash investment in the land was nearly zero, and even his investment in the land in labor might not be large; rather than pay for land he might prefer to move on, if challenged.

These types of illegal occupancy of land went through some interesting developments during the colonial and national history. At first these illegal occupancies were looked upon as trespass, pure and simple—as they would have been in England. Laws and edicts against such occupancy were handed down; sporadic efforts were made to enforce them, but against considerable odds, since such uses typically were along the distant and often unsafe frontier. Through the long land history, these illegal settlers or users came first to be tolerated and then to be favored. In the early colonial days, these unauthorized land occupiers along the frontier came to play a valuable role, as a buffer against the Indian, and often as an advance warning post. These services, plus the aura of adventure and romance they acquired, tended to make heroes out of these frontiersmen. Their crime of using or taking land not theirs was lightly regarded on a frontier where land was plentiful, and their disdain of government was often admired by more staid settlers.

Repeated pleas were made for special favors for the adventurers who went into new territory, "developing" the country and helping to subdue the Indian. Shortly after the new nation was formed, special legislation began to be advocated to favor these frontier settlers. First in special laws, after 1840 in general laws, the virtues of the illegal occupier were placed in higher regard than his sins, and he was given preferential treatment in the disposition of public land. We shall return to this story in more detail in Chapter 8.

CONFLICTS WITH INDIANS

In Chapter 3 we mentioned the problems the very earliest settlers encountered with the American Indians, and particularly the widely differing concepts of land ownership and land use held by the colonists and by the Indians. Most of the colonies experienced open warfare with Indians before many decades. The kind of uncontrolled and illegal entry into new territory by the whites, which we have just

45

described, almost invariably worsened relations between white and red men. Time and again a colony or the federal government would make a treaty or bargain with some group of Indians, only to have some explorers or settlers of the type we have described violate the agreement. The Indians naturally felt betrayed, and they retaliated as best they could. They conducted wars and raids against the white settlements, killing, burning, looting; and the whites retaliated in kind. Although the contest was a relatively equal one during the colonial period and perhaps afterward, in time the sheer weight of white numbers and military equipment was too much for the Indians. In spite of great bravery, and in spite of occasional victories, they were gradually pushed westward and later onto special reservations. Their land became available for white settlement and use. As we have noted, it would have been impossible for the white man's culture and economy to develop and at the same time for the red man to continue his former way of life. The latter was doomed, once the white man became successfully established in what is now the United States.

CHAPTER 6

Origins of the Public Domain

The next major part of our story relates how most of the land within the United States became the property of the federal government; that is the subject of this chapter. Following this step, we will be in a position to relate how that government disposed of most of it; later chapters will relate that story.

At the time of the American Revolution, all the colonies owned some land within their present borders, and in addition several had large land claims outside those borders. Six of the colonies—Maryland, Delaware, Pennsylvania, New Jersey, Rhode Island, and New Hampshire—claimed no land outside their boundaries. But New York, Virginia, North Carolina, South Carolina, Massachusetts, and Connecticut did have such claims. Some of these claims were very large. Virginia, for instance, asserted title to all land lying west and northwest from its shoreline, without limit to the westward. Moreover, the claims of these various states overlapped to a degree.

A number of factors led these colonies, soon to be states, to cede their land to the common government. For one thing, the colonies without land claims insisted upon it, as a price of their entry into the Union. These colonies were fearful of the ultimate size and domination of the colonies with land claims; they wanted a reasonable measure of equality among the various states, as to size and population. There was also strong sentiment for using the revenues from land sales to repay the debts incurred in

47

the common war enterprise. By ceding their claims to the new national government, the separate colonies avoided the problem of deciding as to the validity of conflicting claims.

Cessation of these land claims began before independence had actually been achieved. In 1781, New York ceded its claim to about 200,000 acres in what is now northwestern Pennsylvania. Other colonies or states followed: Virginia in 1784, Massachusetts in 1785, Connecticut in 1786, South Carolina in 1787, North Carolina in 1790, and Georgia in 1802. Some of these states reserved certain lands for their soldiers or for other citizens. In the case of North Carolina, the reserved lands in what is now Tennessee absorbed almost the whole of its claims. For others, the reserved portions were smaller.

In Chapter 8 we shall describe in detail the story of how these and other lands were disposed of by the new federal government. At this point we shall say only that measures for their disposal were passed very early in 1785 and 1787, while the new nation was still under the Articles of Confederation, before the Constitution was adopted. One very important provision of this early legislation was for the later creation of new states from the ceded lands; these new states were to be admitted on terms of complete equality with the older states. In this way, the basis for a union of separate and equal states was established.

By these cessions of colonies and states, the new national government acquired title to all land outside the original thirteen colonies, except that which was already in private ownership. Most of the land from Ohio through Illinois, and up into Michigan and Wisconsin, thus became the property of the federal government. So did the greater part of Alabama and Mississippi, and a much smaller part of Tennessee. The area thus acquired was substantial, although only a small part of the ultimate federal land ownership.

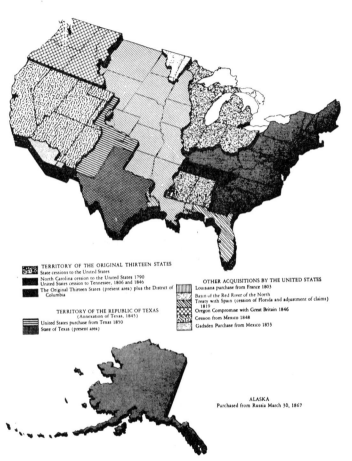

TERRITORY OF THE ORIGINAL THIRTEEN STATES
State cessions to the United States
North Carolina cession to the United States 1790
United States cession to Tennessee, 1806 and 1846
The Original Thirteen States (present area) plus the District of Columbia

TERRITORY OF THE REPUBLIC OF TEXAS
(Annexation of Texas, 1845)
United States purchase from Texas 1850
State of Texas (present area)

OTHER ACQUISITIONS BY THE UNITED STATES
Louisiana purchase from France 1803
Basin of the Red River of the North
Treaty with Spain (cession of Florida and adjustment of claims) 1819
Oregon Compromise with Great Britain 1846
Cession from Mexico 1848
Gadsden Purchase from Mexico 1853

ALASKA
Purchased from Russia March 30, 1867

FIG. 11.—ACQUISITIONS

The area within the present fifty states was acquired by treaty and by purchase from various other countries.

Some of our best farm lands lie in these states, and so do many large and medium-size cities. Most important of all, it was the precedent set by federal acquisition of these lands which was to dominate all later land history in the United States. In this respect, these lands are similar to the history of land tenures in Britain before colonization, for in each case new ideas arose, and precedents were set which largely governed later actions.

LOUISIANA PURCHASE

A dramatic change in the extent of United States territory arose in 1803, when President Jefferson purchased the vast Louisiana Territory from France. A particularly valuable portion of that territory was New Orleans and the control it gave to traffic on the Mississippi River. This was well before the first railroads, and the vast inland areas could be developed only as water transportation of their products was possible. An important route was down the Mississippi. Louisiana had been in Spanish hands and had been taken over only a few years before by France; that country had its hands so full with European wars, so feared its inability to retain Louisiana, and so needed money that it accepted Jefferson's offer of $15,000,000. With interest, settlement of private land claims, and other costs the total was ultimately to reach $27,000,000. While this seems a modest sum these days, for those times it was an enormous sum. With our present-day national income and federal budget, a sum of perhaps $100 billion would be comparable. Most of this land was a wilderness, with no permanent settlers and most imperfectly known. Moreover, Jefferson moved to buy this land without advance congressional approval. If some modern President, from Truman to Eisenhower to Kennedy, were to buy Antarctica for $100 billion, you can have some idea of what an enormous step the Louisiana Purchase was.

As a real estate deal, the Louisiana Purchase was a good bargain. Although land was relatively cheap in those days, yet this purchase price was about 5 cents per acre. Considering how these lands developed over the next one hundred years, this was a low price. As a political deal, it was sheer genius. It almost wholly removed France from the western hemisphere, and it helped set the stage for the Monroe Doctrine a few years later. Moreover, by buying this land, it greatly reduced the likelihood of any other European power getting a new foothold on North America.

Out of the lands so purchased have been created all or parts of thirteen states—Louisiana, Arkansas, Missouri, Iowa, Minnesota, North Dakota, South Dakota, Nebraska, Kansas, Oklahoma, Colorado, Wyoming, and Montana. At one stroke of the pen, the total area of the United States was almost doubled. Although there were some private land claims in this territory, which were honored, nearly all the land became property of the federal government, which has disposed of it in ways we shall consider in Chapter 8.

FLORIDA PURCHASE

Not many years after the Louisiana Purchase—in 1819, to be exact—Spain sold to the United States what is now Florida. Spain had not been very successful in settling Florida, and it was moved by some of the same considerations that led France to sell Louisiana—fear of losing it by war, among others. On the part of the United States, this removed another foreign power from that part of the continent which we were coming to think of as ours, and moreover it removed a source of friction, for border incidents had been common. The War of 1812, which intervened between the Louisiana and Florida purchases, had demonstrated the new country's determination and ability to defend its territory.

TEXAS

Texas came to the United States in a rather unusual way —by treaty. It was an independent country which gave up its independence to join a larger union. Texas had been part of Mexico. Americans began settling there in modest numbers after 1821. Conflict with Mexican authorities led to armed revolt in 1836, and to Texan independence. While the new nation wanted to join the United States at once, arguments over slavery in the Congress held up acceptance of the treaty until 1845. During those years, Texas was an independent republic. As such, it was able to negotiate somewhat about the terms on which it entered the Union. One requirement insisted upon by Texas, and accepted by the United States, was that the land within Texas should belong to the state, not to the federal, government. Thus there has never been any federal public domain in Texas, and the long disposal history we shall examine in Chapter 8 does not apply to Texas. However, that state sold or gave away its lands in a manner rather similar to the processes followed in the public domain states.

When Texas was admitted as a state, there was some uncertainty over its boundaries, especially in the more remote parts. In 1850, the United States bought from Texas its claims to nearly 79 million acres of land, lying in the present states of New Mexico, Colorado, Kansas, Wyoming, and Oklahoma. This land then became part of the public domain, and it has been subject to the operation of laws applicable to other public domain.

PACIFIC NORTHWEST

The United States and Britain each sought to obtain the Pacific Northwest, by settlement and by exploration. During the period 1818 to 1844, we agreed upon joint settlement and joint control. The latter became unsatisfactory to our settlers, for in fact the Hudson's Bay Company largely dominated. As our settlers became more numerous, they demanded clearer title to the United States. Following some acrimonious arguments with Britain, in 1846 we signed a treaty which gave us the present states of Washington, Oregon, and Idaho, and parts of Montana and Wyoming.

PACIFIC SOUTHWEST

Although we annexed Texas in 1845, Mexico was not fully reconciled to its loss. On our side, we were determined to obtain the Pacific Southwest, including California. Some historians regard our war with Mexico as deliberately provoked by us, so that we could thus obtain the territory we wanted and that it was unwilling to sell. At any rate, we declared war on Mexico in 1846, and soon sharply and decisively defeated it. As part of the peace treaty, we obtained the present states of California, Nevada, and Utah, and large parts of Arizona, New Mexico, Colorado, and Wyoming. We did, however, pay for this land at a price per acre roughly the same as we had paid more than 40 years before for the Louisiana Territory.

In the case of both Pacific Northwest and Southwest, the land became the property of the federal government—public domain, subject to disposal under the applicable land laws. A relatively few private land claims existed, which were recognized.

ALASKA

Our last large territorial acquisition was Alaska, which we bought from Russia in 1867. As we noted earlier, the

Russians had early explored the northern Pacific Coast. Their interest had been chiefly in furs. They established a few forts and semipermanent establishments, but virtually no agriculture, for most of the area explored was unsuited to agriculture. With the sea otter, a chief fur species, nearly extinct, and with other fur sources depleted, Russia was willing to sell. There was much criticism within the United States over the purchase—it was widely called "Seward's Folly," from the name of the Secretary of State who negotiated the purchase. Today, of course, we are very glad that Russia is not quite so close to our doorstep. Alaska has produced much wealth as furs, fish, gold, and other minerals. During and since the Second World War, it has been an important defense base.

The land in Alaska, except for very small private land claims, became public domain. Although generally open to disposal under the various land laws, with some special laws applying only to Alaska, very little land had passed out of public ownership up to the time the state was admitted to the Union in 1959.

OTHER AREAS

We acquired several other pieces of national territory, by various ways, some of which became public domain and some of which did not. In 1853, the Gadsden Purchase from Mexico gave us a strip of land across southern New Mexico and Arizona. Title problems were particularly vexatious for part of western Louisiana, for the Red River Valley in North and South Dakota and Minnesota, and for a piece of central Colorado. In this brief treatment, we cannot go into detail about them; each was settled in the end by treaty, and each became public domain.

In a different category were lands which we acquired by treaty or war, but that were never public domain in the sense that the public land laws applied to them. Hawaii was an independent nation which joined the United States at its own request. Puerto Rico, Guam, and the Virgin Islands all became United States possessions, the first two as a result of the war with Spain. We have also governed the Philippine Islands, but these are now an independent nation; and at various times in the past we have governed Cuba. But the public land laws of the United States have never applied to any of these possessions.

CHAPTER 7

Land Survey, Titles, and Records

Dependable titles are basic to any system of private land ownership. As we shall note in Chapter 11, these are largely lacking in Latin America today, and this lack is the cause of much confusion, uncertainty, and conflict. Those of us who believe in democracy also believe that private ownership of land is essential to a democracy. Land titles are one of the things we take for granted in the United States. If we buy a house, we assume that our title to the land on which it sets is secure; often we do not inquire into the details of the land title, assuming that the person who sold it to us owned it clearly and without limitation. However, even in our country, the system of land titles is extremely important, and it is not a matter that we should take for granted.

LAND SURVEY

Before the new government of the United States could dispose of its lands, it had to survey them. As we noted in Chapter 4, different systems of land survey had existed in the colonies. In New England, the town boundaries were surveyed by the colony, and the farms and fields within the town were surveyed by the settlers. While these surveys were crude, at least all the land was surveyed under one common system, and the boundaries of one tract coincided with the boundaries of its neighbor. In the southern colonies, each settler was allowed to select his land as he chose; he was supposed to have it surveyed and to file the survey with a public official. Sometimes he failed to have the survey made. More seriously, this system of selecting land led to gaps between surveys, with small irregular tracts left unselected, and it often led to overlaps and conflicts.

The matter of land survey occupied the Continental Congress, and later the United States under the Articles of Confederation, and still later the Congress. Several issues were debated in those days, for the members of Congress were acutely aware of the great importance of accurate and dependable land surveys. We shall not try to trace these arguments, but we shall describe the land survey system which emerged. It was applied, with only minor local modifications, to all the public domain described in Chapter 6. While Texas was never part of the public domain, similar survey systems were applied there also. Canada, especially in the western provinces, has also used a similar system.

The dominant land survey system is one of rectangular survey. A starting point for an area as large as a state or larger is chosen, often the top of a prominent hill. This point is carefully marked. Through this point is run a north-south line, called the principal meridian; and another line is run east and west, called the base line. On these lines at intervals of six miles are established township lines, thus leading to the creation of six-mile squares called townships. These in turn are divided into 36 sections, each one mile square, or with 640 acres in each. These in turn are divided into quarters, and often the quarters further into quarters or smaller tracts. In this system, each starting point has a name, such as the Mt. Diablo base and meridian; townships are described according to their distance and direction from the starting point, such as township 2 south, range 3 west, or township 6 north, range 9 east. Within each township the sections are numbered, from 1 to 36. The quarters of the section are described according to their position within

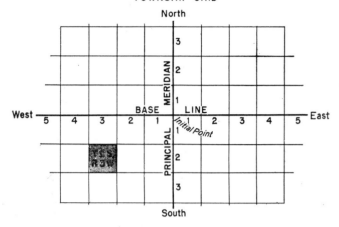

- TOWNSHIP GRID -

TOWNSHIP 2 SOUTH, RANGE 3 WEST

6	5	4	3	2	1
7	8	9	10	11	12
18	17	16	15	Section 14	13
19	20	21	22	23	24
30	29	28	27	26	25
31	32	33	34	35	36

SECTION 14

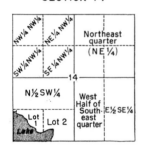

Fig. 12.—Generalized Diagram of the Rectangular System of Surveys

A basic feature of the rectangular system of land surveys is an "initial point." Through this is run a "base line," from east to west, and a "principal meridian," from north to south. Ranges are measured east and west, and townships north and south. Thus the shaded block in the upper diagram in Township 2 South, Range 3 West—or T. 2 S., R. 3 W., for short. This township is six miles on a side, or contains 36 square miles. It is subdivided into 36 "sections" containing one square mile or 640 acres each, as shown in the lower left diagram. The section may be further subdivided as shown in the lower right diagram.

the section, as NW 1/4, or SE 1/4; and similarly, the quarters of the quarters are described according to their position within the quarter.

The results sound like gibberish to the layman: SE 1/4 of NW 1/4, Section 11, Township 3 north, range 5 west, Willamette base and meridian, for instance. But to anyone even moderately familiar with land surveys, this positively identifies a 40-acre tract of land in western Oregon. No other tract of land in the whole United States has this description; no other description can be given to this tract. It is positive, both for this piece of land, and as excluding every other piece of land.

In practice this system encountered many problems. First of all, Congress had specified that the lines of townships were to run true north and south, following the lines of longitude, and true east and west, following lines of latitude, but also that the townships and sections were to be exactly square. This is impossible, since the world is round, and lines parallel to longitude converge as one goes northward. In practice this problem was met by having the township lines run as specified, with most sections exactly square, but all the adjustment thrown into the line of sections across the north and along the west of each township.

Other and more serious operating problems arose as this survey system was applied. Survey should have preceded settlement, but this often meant Indian trouble. Many surveys were crudely done, with many errors; some were fraudulent, and others suspected of being so but never discarded. Section and township corners were supposed to be marked permanently, but in many cases the materials used rotted away relatively soon. Surveys were performed by private contractors until 1910, after which they were taken over by government engineers. Better equipment and more permanent metal markers make modern surveys much better than the old ones.

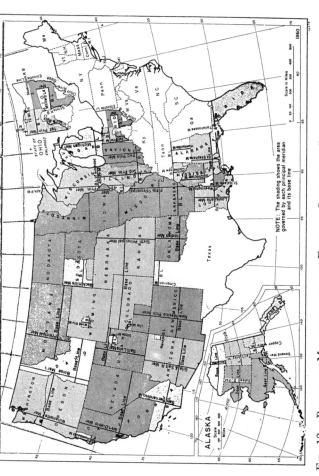

Fig. 13.—Principal Meridians of the Federal System of Rectangular Surveys

All land within each shaded area can be readily and simply described in relation to the "initial point" through which the respective "principal meridian" runs. The most important item in any legal description of land is the base and meridian within which the rest of the description falls. Not all of the western United States and little of Alaska has been surveyed.

In spite of some deficiencies, the survey system under which the public domain was conveyed to private ownership is one of the best in the world, and it is part of our whole system of private property ownership.

A LASTING MARK

The original land survey has left an indelible mark upon those parts of the United States to which it was applied. We are a rectangular country, divided into squares and oblongs like a haphazard checkerboard, with the lines running directly north–south and east–west. You may be somewhat aware of this if you travel by auto in the Middle West or Great Plains, but it comes dramatically to life when you fly. The next time you fly over states established out of the public domain, notice how all-pervading is the original land survey system. You can see mile squares, often with a road on each side; sometimes the square is clearly broken into halves, quarters, or some other fraction; sometimes land from one square is united with that from another in a single farm or forest, somewhat breaking the regular pattern. A modern jet travels about 10 miles per minute, or 600 miles per hour; watch the countryside slide out from under the wing if you are back of the wing (or slide under the wing, if you are seated forward), and count slowly to 6, which is equal to six seconds or one mile. In this way, you can identify the mile-apart section lines. Occasionally you will note a slight jog in a section line; this is probably a township line in which the correction made necessary by the curvature of the earth occurs.

The original land survey has left a more immediate mark on the land than you can see from the air. Roads typically follow the east-west and north-south section lines, even though this means going up and down hills rather than around them. Farmers tend to lay out their fields parallel

61

to the boundaries of their land, even though this may mean cultivating up and down rather than around the slope. Much erosion has been created or accelerated in this way. Some land experts, observing these types of bad land use, have been highly critical of the rectangular land survey. With the knowledge that comes with hindsight, today we can point out ways in which the rolling prairie or forest areas might have been subdivided more along natural drainage lines, thus promoting better land use. But it is far from clear that anyone had the necessary knowledge to do this when the lands were first surveyed.

The advantages of a positive system of land identification, with one and only one description for each tract of land, and with one and only one tract answering to a given description, are very great. Perhaps a rectangular system with a larger net, such as lines every three miles, and with irregular but topographically controlled interior lines, could have been possible and would have had the advantages of both survey systems. But this is all an adventure in "supposing"; we do have the rectangular survey system, its results are very much upon the land, and it has very great virtues.

LAND RECORDS

Not only must land be surveyed, but an adequate system of land records must be kept. The federal government kept a system of land records for the public domain, until each piece of property went into private ownership. The early records are quaint by modern standards, but they served their purpose very well. The land titles of more than half of all privately owned land in the United States today trace back to those early records. Frequently, even today, it is necessary to go back to those records, to be sure that a piece of land actually is in private ownership. Not infrequently flaws in title are discovered, and rather complicated legal procedures are necessary to cure these flaws. Most land records are kept in county offices, however. Land titles are recorded there, and each change in title is also recorded. These records are kept by little known but very important public servants.

When you buy a piece of property today, ordinarily a title abstracter "searches" the title, looking for flaws, and ordinarily he insures to you a perfect title, in return for your payment of a fee to him. This means that he guarantees to defend your title in court, if need be. Some abstracters search through county and other records, to be sure there is a clear line of title from the first holder right down to the person from whom you are buying. In this process, he necessarily subjects the county records to thorough checks and double checks, so that errors in the latter are sooner or later ferreted out. Many of the flaws are quite unimportant—a man forgot to make a will, or transferred a property to a son without proper legal papers, and the like.

Throughout our history, disputes over land titles have been taken to the courts for settlement. Although our courts are far from perfect, and although lawsuits cost so much that they are not a very practical answer for poor men, yet on the whole our courts have operated to make land titles secure. One who asserts a title not in accordance with the available records has to prove his case in court, if he can.

Today it is very rare that a person who follows accepted procedures loses property because of defective land title. The whole system works quietly, and on the whole efficiently; many people think it is too costly, yet it does guarantee land titles in nearly all cases.

CHAPTER 8

The Long Era of Public Land Disposal

Disposal of the public domain dominated United States politics and the United States economy, and was a major factor in the national culture, all through the nineteenth century. Debates in Congress and political campaigns often centered upon public land issues; the economic development of the nation was closely linked to the settlement and improvement of the new lands; and the frontier spirit dominated the national life during this entire century.

When the new Union was established in 1788, it owned, or soon would own, roughly 150 million acres of land—an area about the size of Texas. By 1850, through the various land acquisitions described in Chapter 6, the total area ever in public domain had risen to nearly 1.5 billion acres; the maximum area at any one date was 1.2 million acres. These figures must be compared with a total area of the 48 contiguous states of 1.9 billion acres. Thus over two thirds of the total has been public domain at one time or another. Through the nineteenth century we disposed of more than two thirds of the public land, or more than half the total land area of the nation. This was one of the largest and most dramatic real estate transactions of all times. How this was done is the subject of this chapter.

Although we shall focus on changes in land ownership, we must never forget the fact that these land ownership changes reflected major activities in the lives of many people. Not only did they acquire property and dispose of it, but the very kind of economic and social structure of the

64

nation was affected by the land laws and the kind of land tenure we built up during these decades. Several million people were given a superior economic opportunity, many acquired homes for their families, and a few made fortunes. For the nineteenth century, public land history is to a large extent the total of American history. We should not overlook the immense attraction that free or nearly free land had to immigrants from other countries.

LAND SALES

With the achievement of independence, the new nation owned a great deal of land, was heavily in debt, and was saddled with a seriously depreciated currency. "Not worth a Continental" was a phrase coined out of the worthlessness of the money issued during the Continental Congress period. Everyone was agreed that the publicly owned lands should be disposed of to private ownership; the questions were, how fast, and by what means? The argument largely turned around sales of land as a major source of revenue, versus land as a basis for settlement of a landowning, land-farming class. Those who favored sales mostly wanted to sell to large purchasers, and they were either not concerned with the kind of a rural community that would develop, or favored one with large landowners and tenants. The argument has generally been characterized as Hamilton vs. Jefferson; Hamilton favored using land as a source of revenue, Jefferson was concerned to promote a small landholding rural society.

At first, land policy was largely based upon the making of sales, but it gradually moved away from the objective of securing maximum revenue. As is so often the case, much of the controversy was rather meaningless. There was very little demand for the land owned by the federal government, because the states and individual speculators owned so much land, often closer to settlements. It proved impossible to sell much federal land, or to sell any at a good price. Income from land sales was less than 10 per cent of federal revenue until 1814; during the prior years, the most

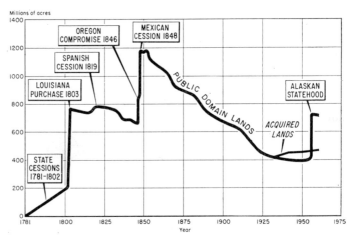

Millions of acres

OREGON COMPROMISE 1846

MEXICAN CESSION 1848

SPANISH CESSION 1819

LOUISIANA PURCHASE 1803

PUBLIC DOMAIN LANDS

ALASKAN STATEHOOD

ACQUIRED LANDS

STATE CESSIONS 1781-1802

Year

FIG. 14.—APPROXIMATE AREA OF FEDERAL LANDS
IN THE UNITED STATES, 1781–1960

The area of federal land within the United States at any time is a result of the balance between land acquisition and land disposal. From 1781 to 1850, land acquisition dominated, and federal holdings reached their peak, at 1,200 million acres, in the latter year. From then until 1930, federal ownership of land declined. Since 1930, federal ownership of land has increased modestly, owing to purchases of land from private citizens. With the admission of Alaska to the Union, federal holdings within the states rose sharply; this land had previously been owned by the federal government, but Alaska was only a territory.

critical in the history of the new nation, land sales produced very little revenue. Land began to sell much more rapidly after this date, and by the middle 1830's land sales accounted for over 40 per cent of national government revenue. They actually created a surplus in the federal treasury; today, with all the talk about deficits, we find it hard to realize that for some years one of the hottest political issues was what to do with the surplus in the federal treasury! Shortly after 1840 the surplus disappeared, never again to reappear; we have been spared that problem in modern times.

Land sales in the 1820's and 1830's were an important part of one of the most speculative eras in American history. There was a speculative fever in the land which centered on buying and selling land. This was a period without a central banking system, and individual banks could, and did, issue money almost to their hearts' content. Paper money was often at a discount, but still it was issued freely, and much of it went into land speculation. The bubble burst in 1837, land prices fell, many people lost their paper fortunes, and the country was plunged into a major economic depression.

During roughly the first half of the nineteenth century, there was a continual struggle between actual settler and land speculator over the terms of federal land sales. The speculators wanted the land offered for sale in the larger cities along the Atlantic seaboard, and in relatively large parcels—several thousand acres in each. The settler wanted the land sold near the frontier, in units of average farm size. Each sought a low price for the land, with easy credit terms. As time went on, methods of selling land gradually shifted in favor of the settler. The minimum unit of sale was gradually reduced from 640 acres in 1796 to 80 acres in 1820, and land offices were gradually opened nearer the land actually being sold. Land prices mostly ranged from $2 per acre downward; this price was higher in those days, relative to prices in general and to incomes, than it was later; yet these prices, in actual dollars per acre, have tended to persist even down to the present. Various experiments were tried with credit, with mostly bad to disastrous results. People agreed to buy land and pay for it on the installment plan, only to find that they could not. Some land reverted for nonpayment, but often a generous Congress forgave debts or extended repayment periods.

Sales of public domain were particularly important during the first half of the nineteenth century, for—except for land warrants based on military service—this was almost the only way of getting federal land. Later, as we shall note below, other means of getting land were made available; but land sales continued long after the other ways were added. The other means were simply added on top of sales, as additional means of disposing of the public domain.

PRE-EMPTION

Pre-emption is an unfamiliar word today, but once it was a major political issue. The struggles over it, and their outcome, illustrate American land history as well as any other single episode.

We noted in Chapter 5 how land settlement tended to run ahead of land survey. There was always some interval after survey before land was actually offered for sale, and settlement took place during this period also. People took up land, cleared the forest from it, erected buildings, and grew crops, all without any legal title to the land. How shall we regard these people: as trespassers, which legally they were, liable to all the penalties imposed on trespassers in more densely settled areas; or as noble pioneers, opening up the land to settlement so that others could follow more safely—which they also sometimes were? When the land was actually offered for sale, should these prior occupants have been forced to bid for the land against anyone who sought it, or should they have been given special preference in acquiring land? As we noted in Chapter 5, sentiment gradually came

68

to support the settler, and the terms of sale were gradually shifted in his favor. The basic issue was the right of a settler to "pre-empt" or to buy the land he sought at a fixed price, without the necessity of competing with others at a sale.

A series of special pre-emption acts were passed, almost from the first cash sales of land, but generally they applied only to certain areas or only for limited periods of time. However, so many such acts were passed that in effect most settlers were protected by them. In 1841, a general Pre-emption Act was passed. It applied only to sale of land which had been settled after land survey, but shortly it was amended to include settlement before survey also. When land was put up for sale, a settler had the right to buy for $1.25 per acre the land which he had settled. He was limited to one entry, not to exceed 160 acres, and he was ineligible if he already owned more than 320 acres of land. These acts were of great help to actual settlers and to small speculators who could take advantage of their terms.

In practice the pre-emption acts were much abused. Men would file claims and assert residence, when in fact they never lived upon the land. They sought to acquire it so that they could sell at a profit to some later actual settler. "Claim clubs," or associations of those asserting settlement claims, were organized. These clubs were often coercive, forcing actual settlers to buy land from them rather than from the federal land office. They were sometimes effective in this endeavor as well as in that of helping to protect the legitimate claims of their members.

LAND GRANTS FOR PUBLIC PURPOSES

The United States government owned a great deal of land, public and private capital was in short supply, and the need for public improvements was great; why not make public land available to finance the construction of needed public improvements? This was a sound basic idea, which accomplished a great deal of good, but which in practice was also seriously abused.

The first, and most important, grants of this type were in support of public schools at the elementary grade level. We do not realize it today, but in the early nineteenth century a large proportion of our population was illiterate, and the demand for free public education was both very great and very daring. The Ordinances of 1785 and 1787, passed during the Confederation period, provided that one section, or 640 acres, of land out of each township would be available to support local public schools. Later, this grant was raised for the states which came into the Union to two and then to four sections. Thus, 3, 6, and 11 per cent, respectively, of the public domain was granted to the states upon their admission to the Union, in support of public schools. If the named sections were already in private ownership, the states were allowed to select "in lieu" lands.

Later states were given other grants, "quantity grants" so called because they were for a stipulated total area rather than for certain named sections in each township, for other public institutions. The most notable of these were for agricultural and mechanical arts colleges, which to this day are known as land grant colleges. But they also supported schools for the blind, mental hospitals, mining schools, and other institutions. The quantity grants were somewhat more valuable because the states were allowed to select the land where they chose. These grants for educational and other purposes were extremely important; they provided a larger public endorsement of the idea for which they were made, they provided a significant part of the original costs, and they provided the impetus to the states to provide the rest of the money from their own sources. Possibly even more important than these specific results, they provided the precedent for a very common feature of federal-state relations today, namely the grant-in-aid.

70

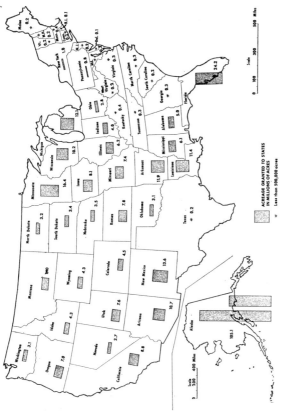

FIG. 15.—FEDERAL LAND GRANTS TO STATES, 1803–1962

One major means by which land was transferred from the federal government was by grants to states. The largest were made to the states with large areas of "swamp" land within their borders, and to some of the states last admitted to the Union, which received larger common school grants. Alaska has received the largest grants of all, both in absolute area and as a proportion of its total area. Some states have retained substantial parts of the land received, but most of it has been sold.

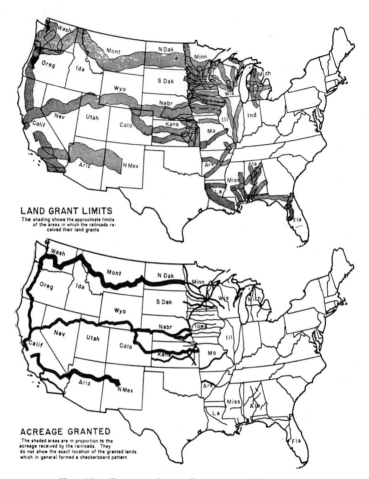

LAND GRANT LIMITS

The shading shows the approximate limits of the areas in which the railroads received their land grants

ACREAGE GRANTED

The shaded areas are in proportion to the acreage received by the railroads. They do not show the exact location of the granted lands, which in general formed a checkerboard pattern

FIG. 16.—FEDERAL LAND GRANTS FOR RAILROADS

The land grants to railroads were ordinarily for alternate sections. The outer limits of the grant areas were relatively wide, partly because much of the land within them was already in private ownership and the railroads were able to select only the open public domain. The areas actually granted, while substantial, were only a small portion of the total area within grant limits.

The states were the recipients of large grants of swamp and overflow lands. This type of grant was, to put it kindly, based upon a misconception—the assumption that the states somehow could and would reclaim these lands which the federal government either could not or would not reclaim. In fact the states then, as often today, were both financially and technically less able to do this than was the federal government. A great deal of valuable cropland, subject to occasional overflow, was given the states in this way, and by them often sold at very low prices to land speculators with political influence. Much of the Central Valley of California and the Delta of Mississippi went in this way. As we shall see later in this chapter, the acreages involved were substantial.

Another major type of land grant was in aid of transportation. Small grants were made for wagon roads and canals, but large grants were made for railroads. The latter began in 1850 and were largely completed by 1870. The typical grant to aid in railroad construction consisted of alternate sections of land for a specified distance on either side of the rail line; the price of the remaining government sections was then doubled, both to provide the government with as much revenue as it would otherwise have received, and to reflect the fact that these lands were more valuable once rail facilities existed. If the granted land was already in private ownership, in lieu lands could be selected, often within a specified further distance from the rail line. Many railroads sold their lands as fast as they could; others held large acreages for comparatively long periods. In return for the grant, the federal government received special rates on its freight shipped over these rail lines—a concession that produced something in excess of $1 billion in reduced freight fares to the federal government, until this provision was repealed in 1940 and 1945. Many arguments have raged over who won the best of the bargain, the federal government or the railroads. At any rate, this was an important means of transferring land from public to private ownership.

THE HOMESTEAD ACT AND
ITS SUCCESSORS

The agitation over land for settlers by no means ended with the passage of the Pre-emption Act in 1841. But for the next twenty years, public land matters were inextricably mixed with the struggle over the extension or restriction of slavery. Those from the slave states who feared they would be outvoted by the free states sought to promote systems of landholdings which would favor the extension of slavery; those who sought to contain slavery sought land systems which would make it unprofitable. Efforts were made, but failed, to pass a general homestead law during these two decades.

In 1862, with the southern states out of Congress, a Homestead Act was passed. While this has been widely hailed as unique, yet in fact it was but the extension of land disposal systems that had been in effect for some time; it did not replace sale and grant disposal but merely supplemented them. It permitted a citizen, or a person who had declared his intention of becoming one, to enter upon as much as 160 acres of land; after five years' residence and making certain improvements, he was permitted to obtain final title on payment of $1.25 per acre. The latter was no lower than land had been offered for sale previously, and was higher than some land was available for. But the act did extend an open invitation to settlers to enter on the land and improve it, and it did assure title if these conditions were lived up to.

Several later laws followed this general pattern. The Timber Culture Act in 1873 provided that a person could obtain 160 acres of land if he would plant trees on 40 acres of it—later changed to 10 acres. This act was widely perverted. Trees were planted in regions where there was no hope of their growing; it is even reported that grain farmers sowed tree seeds with their wheat, so that they could swear they had "planted" trees—and was it their fault if the wheat grew and was harvested, and the trees did not grow? The settler had only to plant trees, no record of success in growing them being necessary. Under the Desert Land Act, passed in 1878, a settler could get 640 acres of land (later reduced to 320), if he would irrigate one eighth of it. This act was subjected to numerous frauds also. The area obtainable under a homestead was increased to 320 acres in 1909 and to 640 acres in 1916, as settlement extended to drier and drier areas; and residence was reduced from five to three years in 1912. The Carey Act provided for grants to states for their irrigation of the land and for essentially a homestead system on the reclaimed lands. The federal Reclamation Act was passed in 1902, providing for federal irrigation projects. Although it had been expected that most of the land so irrigated would be public domain, in practice most of it has become privately owned.

SUMMARY OF LAND DISPOSAL

Some idea of the relative importance of the various methods of land disposal can be gained from a few statistics. For the 48 contiguous states, the area in millions of acres is given in Figure 17.

Total Land Area	1,904
Original Public Domain	1,442
Total Disposition, All Methods	1,031
Cash Sales, and Miscellaneous Methods	300
Homesteads	285
Grants to States	225
Military Bounties and Private Claims	95
Railroad Grants	91
Timber Culture and Other Related Acts	35

FIG. 17.—METHODS OF LAND DISPOSAL

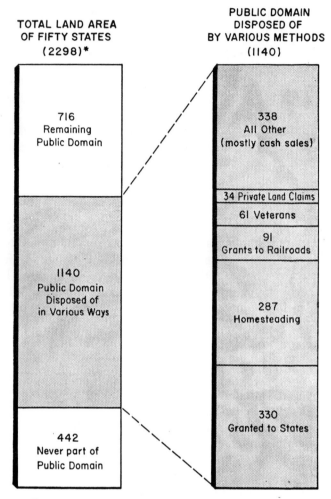

*Figures in millions of acres.

FIG. 18.—PUBLIC DOMAIN AND ITS DISPOSAL

Most land in the United States was once public domain. Half of the entire national area was once public domain but has been disposed of. States were granted a large portion of it; other large areas were sold or homesteaded, but a variety of disposal methods were employed.

In considering these statistics, you should recall that an average state, such as Illinois or Iowa, has about 35 million acres of total area. California, our second largest state, has about 100 million acres of total area.

The area of land disposed of by a particular method is not necessarily the only or best measure of its importance. Some methods were available early, when better quality land was available; others came into operation later, when the land was drier and generally less productive. Other features of the laws, such as the regulation of the area that could be obtained in a single transaction, were also important.

We have made no mention thus far of disposals under the mining laws. While these were very important in some situations, the total area was small relative to the areas under other methods. The complexities of the mining laws are very great and extend to the present day, but in this short volume we cannot include them in our discussion.

ALASKA

This chapter has thus far excluded Alaska. As we noted in earlier chapters, the total area of that state is 365 million acres. From 1867 until Alaska was admitted to the Union in 1959, only about 1 million acres had passed from federal to private ownership. In very large part, this is simply because land is not the basis of most of the economy of Alaska. The new state was given a very large grant, far larger than any state up to that point, which may ultimately reach 100 million acres or more. In general, most disposal laws have applied to Alaska, and in addition some special ones have applied there only.

TRESPASS, FRAUD, SPECULATION, AND WASTE

The more than century long disposal of public lands was a lusty, brawling, rowdy affair. Valuable lands were put up for sale, first come first served, with only modest rules, and those often not enforced fully. Men with drive, desire for land, ability to cope with the frontier, or with modest capital, sought to improve their economic position for themselves and their families either by getting a farm or by making money in land dealings. It was like a vast grab bag at a party, with valuable gifts for those who could get them and hold them. And, as probably would be true at such a party today, there were always some who sought to shove in ahead of others, to snatch particularly valuable prizes, or otherwise to beat the rules. Trespass, fraud, speculation, and waste were rampant; but in the process a nation was built.

As we noted in Chapter 5, many people occupied or used land without shadow of legal title and without permission. Oftentimes this illegal occupancy did little damage to the land, harmed no one, and in time ended when the trespasser or someone else acquired the land from the federal government. But timber trespass was a different story. This kind of trespass involved someone harvesting all the merchantable timber from government land and selling it for his own profit; the land was left denuded, often regenerated as forest slowly or not at all, and all the value of the land was gone so that no one was interested in buying or acquiring it. This type of trespass was common, especially in the Lake States; many a large fortune was made or begun in this way. Grazing trespass was common throughout the West and ended only with the establishment of national forests and grazing districts, which we will discuss in Chapter 9. Grazing trespass often involved overgrazing; more

78

seriously, it usually involved improper seasonal grazing, which is even more destructive. In the process, the productivity of range lands was seriously impaired. The early mining in the West lacked any legal sanction in federal law, although miners often established a type of local law. In all of these and in other ways, trespass was common on the public domain.

In the process of acquiring title to land, many individuals practiced outright frauds. One of the most fertile of such sources was the private land claim. When we bought the Louisiana Purchase or other areas or acquired territory by treaty, recognition of the existing private land claims was always included. Such claims were often hazy; titles or deeds were often imprecise, and surveys often nonexistent. This offered a great opportunity for fraud, and it was eagerly seized upon. Many asserted claims were denied, and many granted when there was great suspicion that the claims were fraudulent. The settlement requirement for use of pre-emption was another common source of fraud; claimants would assert settlement when no one could find any evidence of it on the ground. The matter of improvements on homesteads was another common source of fraud; men would assert they had made certain improvements, when in fact they had not. These various frauds were outright dishonesty, but they were generally condoned in the times. The standards of business and other conduct were different from those today, and many people believed it perfectly proper to cheat the government—and some still do, we must confess. While much fraud was uncovered, those practicing it were rarely punished seriously; and lack of necessary manpower, plus lack of court support, often made it difficult to uncover and prove much of the fraud suspected of existing.

In this connection, we should realize that the Congress itself was very tender with land claimants. Many congressmen were themselves speculators or dealers in land. Many of the unproven, probably fraudulent private land claims were verified by special congressional action; time and again, when some group of settlers had not complied with the law, Congress would enact special legislation freeing them of their original obligation. Congress was never willing to give the General Land Office the size and kind of staff needed to uncover and prove fraud. In acting thus, Congress then—as now—was reflecting the wishes of most of its constituents. As a nation, we did not wish to spoil the grab-bag party by too strict insistence on the rules.

Speculation in lands, especially in land recently public land, was ubiquitous through the nineteenth century. Everyone did it; a large measure of it was unavoidable, given the circumstances of the times. Even the most altruistic settler risked much, including his life and that of his family, when he sought to carve a farm out of the frontier wilderness. But there were many men whose concern was land speculation, who never thought of settling on frontier land themselves. Many of our national leaders, from George Washington on down, bought and sold land for profit. Many fortunes were made, but not everyone won in this game. Naturally, speculators sought maximum gains with minimum involvement of their own capital, and one of the best ways of doing this was to speculate in public land, to which one could assert some kind of claim but which did not require large amounts of capital. Many arguments have raged over the degree to which, if at all, the land speculator performed a valuable public service. His apologists have pointed out that he often received title to land in tracts of sizes sufficient to warrant settlers buying from him rather than from the government. Moreover, governmental land processes were often slow and sometimes uncertain, whereas the land speculator could often deliver title quickly. Most people, however, have argued that the speculator was more nearly a parasite, living off the productive efforts of others and contributing little himself.

The land disposal process was also a wasteful one. Speculation is always waste, for it diverts productive energies and talents away from more productive processes. Much land settlement involved waste, for settlers tried to establish farms under such conditions that failure was almost inevitable. A great many settlers tried to farm land suitable only for grazing, for instance. Many years of effort often ended in failure, and some accumulated capital was lost in the process. The whole settlement process was one of trial and error, with plenty of the latter.

But the land disposal process was an essential part of building a nation. One need not endorse every step taken to assert that the end product was magnificent. In little more than a century the United States had developed from a fringe along the Atlantic Coast to a continental nation, vastly larger in population as well as in area, and with highly productive farms, forests, and mines. Perhaps the process could have been more orderly, with the wisdom that comes of hindsight; but the qualities that made the pioneer willing to push out onto the frontier were impatient of restraint, and it may be doubted if a slower and better controlled land disposal system would have been acceptable to the nation at the time.

81

CHAPTER 9

Permanent Reservation of Federal Land for Public Use

The wholesale headlong process of land disposal has had some critics throughout its history; as time went on their voices grew stronger, and in the end these critics initiated actions which materially changed the whole concept of land ownership and use. From colonial times onward, some men had been disturbed by the "wearing out" of farm land, its abandonment, and the clearing of new land to take its place. Later the indiscriminate destruction of forests disturbed many other men. A major national shock occurred in 1880, when the Census of Agriculture revealed that a fourth of all farmers were tenants; a nation proud of its independent landowning farmers discovered it had many who were but tenants on other men's land.

One major outcome of this dissatisfaction with the land disposal process was the reservation of some federal land for permanent public ownership and for public use. The history of this movement is the subject of this chapter; in Chapter 12 we shall consider how the public lands are managed.

The reversal of indiscriminate land disposal and the substitution of permanent reservation of some land was definitely an intellectual process. A few of the intelligentsia and a few public figures saw the need and the opportunity, and they maneuvered public action in the direction they sought. At the time there was little public knowledge of the situation, and less public appreciation of need and opportunity. Later general public support developed, until today the kinds of federal lands we shall discuss in this chapter are strongly supported by the electorate and the public generally.

NATIONAL PARK SYSTEM

The beginnings of any social change are notoriously hard to pinpoint; it is always possible to point to some earlier action, either similar or that paved the way for a specific change. Various reservations of public domain had been made for public purposes during the first half of the nineteenth century and even earlier. Some reservations without clear public purpose were also made; and some areas reserved at relatively early dates were much later incorporated into permanent reservations. But the area usually considered as the first permanent federal land reservation was Yellowstone National Park, established in 1872. The area had been explored by various official and semiofficial parties in the immediately preceding years, and the accounts of this unusual region aroused much public interest. A special Act of Congress reserved and withdrew the area from settlement and disposition under the land laws, to be "set apart as a public park or pleasuring ground for the benefit and enjoyment of the people." The act gave the Secretary of the Interior the power to manage the area and to prescribe rules to this end.

It was clear as the years rolled by that neither the people nor the Congress had a clear idea what a national park was, or how it was to be managed. At first, Yellowstone was very hard to get to. Its reservation from disposal under the land laws meant little at first, for there probably would have been little or no demand for this remote land at that time anyway. Congress was very miserly at first with appropriations for its management. Hunters and game poachers killed much of the game. Only gradually were laws and rules enacted prohibiting such practices, and still more slowly were they stamped out. Later there were numerous proposals to log its timber, or dam its major river to create an irrigation storage dam, or otherwise to use it in ways that today we realize are incompatible with national park management. The park came to be better known about the time of the First World War, and in the years intervening

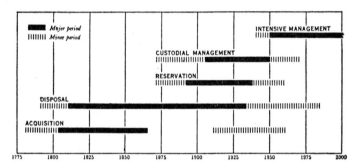

FIG. 19.—MAJOR ERAS IN FEDERAL LAND OWNERSHIP AND
LAND MANAGEMENT IN THE UNITED STATES, 1800–2000

The processes of acquisition, disposal, reservation, and management of federal lands have been partly separate and partly overlapping in time.

to the present its use has grown by leaps and bounds, and its popularity and public support have risen accordingly.

Three more national parks were established in 1890: Yosemite, General Grant, and Sequoia, all in California. To these were added Mount Ranier in 1899 and Crater Lake in 1902. These all are unique areas by any standards, and today they are excellent specimens of national parks. Each of these major additions was the subject of special legislation; there was no idea as yet of a national park system.

The popularity of the national park idea was such that three distinctly inferior areas were added to the national park system: Wind Cave in South Dakota, in 1903; Sullys Hill in North Dakota, in 1904; and Platt, in Oklahoma, in 1906. The glories of the first were extolled by congressmen from the region, and their judgments accepted by Congress. There is considerable doubt that Congress intended to establish a national park at Sullys Hill; it did establish a park, kind unspecified, which gradually came to be accepted as a national park. In 1931, it was reclassified as a national game preserve. Platt was also acclaimed by local supporters. The fact that these inferior areas were accepted is the best possible evidence of the lack of a system of national parks, and of clear concepts as to what a national park really is. The administration of the parks was then so poor that there was no one to speak against such inferior areas, and no standards existed by which to judge them.

A long list of national parks was added thereafter, beginning with Mesa Verde in 1906 and ending with Virgin Islands and Petrified Forest parks in 1956 and 1958. Far more important than these additions in themselves was the passage in 1916 of an act establishing the National Park Service and for the first time setting forth the concept of a system of national parks. National parks still must be established by special act of Congress, and each candidate must be truly outstanding to be accepted. But now there are standards, admittedly somewhat subjective in character, for inclusion in the system.

In 1906 an act was passed providing for national monuments, which can be established by presidential proclamation. There are nearly one hundred of these today. They fall into five general groups: remains of prehistoric civilizations, historic relics, geologic examples, botanic reservations, and wild animal reservations. Although many are small, a few are large. Some areas, set aside as national monuments in the past, have been accepted as national parks when they became better known. There are other kinds of areas in the present-day national park system— national seashores, national military parks, national historic sites, national cemeteries, and others.

Most of the national parks and the larger national monuments were established out of the public domain, either directly or from national forests which in turn had been formed from the public domain. This meant that most of them are in the West, where most of the federal lands lay at the time parks were established. For some parks and other areas, however, states and private citizens have purchased the land and have given it to the United States. This procedure has been more common in the East than in the West. The Rockefeller family has been particularly generous in helping to buy land for this purpose. In 1961, a precedent was established when Congress established the Cape Cod national seashore, with the provision that the federal government buy the land required. Since that date, two other seashores have been established, with similar provisions.

Use of the national parks has risen enormously in recent years, but that story we shall tell in Chapter 12.

NATIONAL FORESTS

National forests are much more extensive than national parks, and in some ways they better exemplify the permanent reservation of federal land for public use. At least, their use is much more varied than is that of the national parks.

Concern over the indiscriminate cutting of forests, including trespass on the public domain and the lack of fire control, led to many proposals for some different form of management of public forested lands. The Department of the Interior, where the administration of such lands lay, tried unsuccessfully for many years to get legislation to this end. Finally in 1891 a provision was inserted in a land bill enabling the President to reserve forest lands. That provision of the bill was added in conference late one night, after different bills, none of which contained this section, had passed Senate and House. The final bill was presented on the last day before Congress adjourned; it was not printed, but passed after a reading by the respective chairmen. As any student of government knows, a single voice in opposition would have been sufficient to raise a point of order and thus strike out a provision added in conference, that had been in no previous bill. There is good reason to believe that the Congress did not know then, or for many years, the potentiality of the law it had passed. This is what we mean by intellectual promotion of public land legislation.

Some forest land was reserved under this act in the next few years. The law had made no provision for use of the land or its products or for any management of the lands. The reservations were paper actions, unenforced on the ground. Nevertheless, and quite properly, there was complaint about the law that locked up valuable resources so they could not be used. In 1897, just before his term ended, President Grover Cleveland withdrew comparatively large areas, arousing much public criticism. One of the first acts of the new Congress and the new President was to pass a law providing for the sale of timber from these lands, and for their use for other purposes. This too was a most unusual legislative maneuver: specific permanent legislation as a rider on an appropriations bill; and it also was subject to a point of order had anyone objected. Although the new legislation has proven over the years since to be adequate, Congress did not for some years reinforce it with significant appropriations.

President Theodore Roosevelt made very extensive reservations of forest land, so large that they aroused so much opposition that Congress passed a law that no more national forests could be established in most western states without its approval. Roosevelt signed the bill into law, but not until he withdrew still larger acreages. One can well imagine the storm of opposition that created! But his action was not overturned. It brought the area of national forests in 1907 up to a level which they were not to exceed for many years, and a level not much lower than their present area. Later some land was eliminated from the national forests, for it was found that in the haste of establishing them some land had been included which was not well suited to this purpose.

President Theodore Roosevelt transferred administration of the national forests from the General Land Office in the Department of the Interior to the new Forest Service in the Department of Agriculture. On the face of it this may seem like a simple administrative change, but it was much more than that. It catapulted into the leadership of the conservation movement the young forester, Gifford Pinchot, whose later bitterly partisan attacks on the Department of the Interior split the conservationists and left scars which have hardly healed to this day. It divided the major land management activities of the federal government between two major departments; in spite of many proposals to recombine them, they still remain divided. This action on Roosevelt's part, like many another administrative action, was taken in part to avoid the messy job of reforming the General Land Office, which was badly needed. Had he chosen instead to have undertaken the latter, either with or without Pinchot as the reformer, and had he been successful, much federal land history would be different.

FEDERAL WILDLIFE REFUGES

When the white man first explored and settled the United States, each particular region was teeming with game, in part because the Indians with their less destructive weapons were unable to kill game as easily as were white men. The original animal population was greatly reduced by hunting and trapping. Beaver, for instance, were trapped in large numbers and exterminated through much of their original range; buffalo were hunted for their skins, the meat being left to rot, until they were reduced from vast numbers to small remnant herds; the passenger pigeon, once unbelievably numerous, was completely exterminated. Many people became concerned about this slaughter and the consequent paucity of game. Yellowstone Park was closed to hunting in 1894, and several states established wildlife refuges before or after that date.

The first federal wildlife refuge was established in 1903. Only a relatively few rather small wildlife reserves were established for many years. Migratory bird treaties were signed in 1916 and in 1937, under which this nation undertook to protect migratory birds while they were in this country. The big expansion of wildlife refuges came under President Franklin D. Roosevelt, partly by setting aside tracts of public domain for this purpose, partly by buying lands for the same objective. Today there is a relatively extensive system of such areas, although additional areas are needed if certain scarce and valuable species are to be preserved. One unusual feature of this program is that duck hunters are required to buy federal stamps in order to be allowed to hunt ducks, and the money obtained thus goes into a fund from which additional refuge areas are purchased.

GRAZING DISTRICTS

In spite of the extensive withdrawals of land for permanent public use areas described above, and in spite of the continued disposal of land to individuals in the ways described in Chapter 8, as late as 1934 there were still over

180 million acres of so-called open public domain—so called because open to entry under the land laws. These were the driest, rockiest, least fertile parts of the original public domain. Land disposal had always been a selective process; each settler or speculator took the most valuable land he knew about that was available. The reservations we have described thus far in this chapter were also a selective process; the best forests were put into national forests, and the most scenic areas into national parks. Most of the remaining public domain in 1934 was suited only for grazing, its productivity even for this use was low, and some of it was too desert even for this use. Although available under some land laws, much of it did not warrant any expenditure in order to acquire title, and much of it could not pay even minimal taxes. All of it that produced enough forage to support domestic livestock was being grazed by such livestock; their owners lacked clear legal rights to do so, but they continued to do so by sufferance. The lands were typically overstocked and used improperly for their seasonal adaptability, and as a result their productivity was impaired below their original low level.

Over the decades many proposals had been made for the essentially grazing lands of the West—their disposal in large enough blocks to meet the needs of ranchers, or their management under some form of public administration. Such proposals began in a serious way as early as 1880; Pinchot nearly succeeded in implementing such an idea shortly after 1900. But all such proposals failed, in part because far too many people misjudged the capacity of such lands, believing them capable of crop production if properly managed. By the 1920's it was becoming increasingly clear that these lands were suited only for grazing, but that some better system of grazing management was needed. A number of bills were introduced in Congress, with increasing probability of passage.

In 1934, the Taylor Grazing Act provided a permanent system of management for these lands. One important feature of the act was the authority to classify lands—something previously wholly lacking in federal land legislation —and to deny disposal except when classified as suitable for the purpose sought. Means were established for selling odd parcels, isolated from the major areas, and for leasing for grazing other small parcels. The major feature of the act, however, was the provision for grazing districts, with licensing of livestock grazing and with a positive program of land management. In practice the grazing districts have been managed in ways generally similar to the national forests; being less productive on the whole, management has been less intensive, with grazing emphasized more and timber harvest less. The remainder of the public domain was under positive management at last!

PURCHASE AND EXCHANGE

The federal government has not only disposed of its public domain. It has also acquired land by purchase and by exchange. The first major purchase program was the Weeks Act, passed in 1911. The first national forests were all in the West, because that is where the public domain lay. Interest in national forests in the East led to the passage of this act, under which more than 20 million acres of land have been purchased since 1911. In one unusual move the government recaptured some lands in Oregon that had been granted to a railroad but the terms of the grant for which had been violated. These lands, known as O & C (from the Oregon and California railroad, never built under this name, but built as part of the Southern Pacific railroad system) contained only about 2.5 million acres, but they were covered with unusually fine timber. Some land had passed to private ownership within the boundaries of na-

91

tional parks, before the parks were established, and some of this land has been purchased.

In the 1930's a different kind of federal land purchase program was established. Its purpose was to buy lands and farms submarginal for continued farm operation, and to convert them to grass or forest. Some national forest lands were acquired in this manner, the federal wildlife refuges received major areas of land in this way, and substantial areas were turned over to states for park purposes. Later, during the Second World War and later, the defense and atomic energy agencies have purchased extensive areas for their needs.

In addition to purchases, the federal government has acquired land through exchanges. Many different types of exchanges are authorized under a variety of laws. There are many difficulties in finding a private landowner who wants to trade one piece of land for another, under terms so that both he and the government have gained. Exchanges are a form of barter—a particularly primitive form, since each side offers the same commodity, land. Before the Second World War, the Forest Service exchanged timber for land, but this type of exchange is no longer made. The total area involved in all types of exchanges is relatively small, but exchanges are sometimes highly important locally. They provide one way that individuals can get land, and also one way that the federal government can acquire lands it wants for particular programs. A more fluid land sale and land purchase program would make it easier for each side to receive satisfaction from these transactions.

CHAPTER 10

Land Ownership Today

The historical processes described in the preceding chapters have produced the pattern of land ownership we find today in the United States; the latter is the subject of this chapter. In later chapters we shall consider in more detail how the various kinds of land are used in the United States today. But an overall view of present land ownership seems necessary at this point.

PUBLIC LANDS

Public lands include land owned by the federal, state, county, city, and other miscellaneous units of government. Of these the acreage owned by the federal government is by far the largest, but some of the most valuable public lands are those owned by cities and other local governments. Unfortunately the available data are almost wholly in terms of land area, and they are frequently inadequate even in this measure; we know very little indeed about the value of public lands.

One third of the entire area of the United States is owned by the federal government; some of it has always been so owned; other large areas have been acquired by purchase from private owners. Almost half of all the federal land is in Alaska, where almost 99 per cent of all the land still belongs to the federal government. In very large part this percentage measures the fact that ownership of land is not

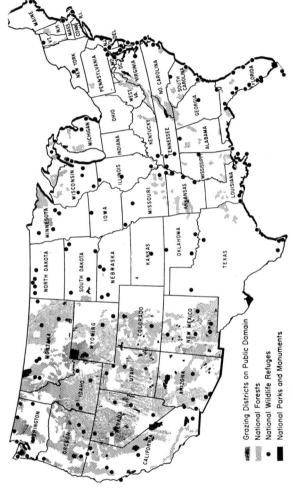

Fig. 20.—Federal Land Area of the Forty-Eight Contiguous States

Over a third of all federal lands lie in Alaska, not shown on this map. A full half of the total lies in the Rocky Mountains and to their westward. This concentration of federal land ownership in certain regions is partly the result of land history, partly because the lands in question are not suited for agricultural uses.

Grazing Districts on Public Domain
National Forests
National Wildlife Refuges
National Parks and Monuments

an important means for economic production in Alaska; very little agriculture is found there, such forestry as has developed is from public lands, mineral development takes little land area, and the same is true for such industrial and commercial development as exists. For the 48 contiguous states, slightly more than one fifth of the total area is federally owned. There is a small area of federal land in Hawaii also.

Of the large federal estate, less than 4 per cent is owned by defense agencies; the rest is owned by various civil agencies. Of these, the Department of the Interior controls almost exactly two thirds of the total federal land; the Department of Agriculture controls about one fourth. The federal lands have been classified by their administering agencies according to the predominant land usage. On this basis, two thirds of the land is predominantly for forests and wildlife; slightly more than a fifth is predominantly for grazing; and miscellaneous uses occupy the remainder. There is not a clear-cut division of lands by usage among the agencies; several agencies may administer land used for several purposes.

The various states also own land. Some of this ownership —about two thirds of the total—is the remainder of their original grants from the federal government; some results from land purchases for special purposes. States other than Alaska were granted about 230 million acres of land; Alaska was given a grant which ultimately could include over 100 million acres, but the area actually transferred to Alaska by 1962 was only a few million acres. The states now own somewhat more than 80 million acres. State land ownership is most common in the western United States, in the same region where federal land ownership is most common.

Cities, counties, and local units of government such as drainage districts also own land. We lack precise and inclusive data on this type of public land ownership. Surprisingly, however, as nearly as we can estimate, the proportion of public land within cities is about the same as public land for the nation at large—one third of the total. We often do not realize the extent of public land ownership in cities. Streets and alleys are publicly owned, and these alone account for a sizable proportion of the total city area. Moreover, they are extremely important, largely because they so strongly influence if not govern the use of private lands. Along with recreation, school, and other special-purpose lands, they include close to one third of the total area of most cities.

FARMS

Over 80 per cent of all private land in the United States is included within farms. This includes far more than the crop and pasture land we usually associate with farms. One third of all commercial forest land is in farms, and about one seventh of the farm area is classified as commercial forest. In addition, relatively large acreages of low-grade grazing land and of noncommercial forest are found within farms.

In 1959 there were 3.7 million farms in the United States, containing in total 1,123 million acres, or an average of 304 acres per farm. The trend for the past few decades has been toward fewer farms and more land in farms. Farm numbers were once as high as 6.5 million, so that the reduction from the peak is more than a third; large-scale further reductions in farm numbers seem highly probable in the next few decades. We may well have no more than a million farms by 2000. Farmers have been increasing the total area of all farms, by including within their definite management control a great deal of grazing land and some forest land that previously had been outside of farms. As a result of these two changes, average acreage per farm has doubled, from 146 acres in 1920 to 304 acres in 1959; if farm numbers continue to decline as suggested above, average farm area will well exceed 1,000 acres by 2000. We hasten to point out that the use of hired labor per farm has also declined over recent decades; on the average, farms today are more nearly single-man farms than they were in earlier decades. The rise in acreage per farm, therefore, is not evidence of a decline in the role of the family farm but rather reflects the ability of the average farmer to operate far more land with today's machinery.

The foregoing discussion relates to the farm as an operating unit, not to the farm as a unit of land ownership. Typically in the past, a farm was owned and operated by the same man, perhaps with some hired labor; such farms were typically bequeathed to the farmer's son, perhaps going through a period of tenancy as the son operated the farm his father owned. But there have always been some tenants, men who operate land owned by another. This was true even in the colonial period, as we noted in Chapter 4. Tenancy gradually became common in the older farm areas; but the really big increase in farm tenancy came after the Civil War, when the freed slaves became sharecroppers. In the last two decades there has been a big increase in the tenure class called "part owners." These are men who own some land and rent some. A man with a farm too small for maximum income often seeks to enlarge it; lacking capital to buy additional land, or hesitant to buy at prices he considers too high, he rents an additional farm or part of one. In 1959 this class of tenure was the second numerous, after full owners, but it included the largest acreage. Full owners numbered over 2 million; the farms they operated averaged 164 acres each, and in addition these farmers rented out to other farmers an average of 17 acres each. Tenants, who rented all their land, numbered about three quarters of a million, with farms averaging 221 acres each.

Part owners, totaling somewhat fewer than 1 million, operated 348 acres of their own and 280 rented acres each, on the average.

Various studies indicate that half or more of the owners of rented farm land are, or were, farmers; some are still active, more have retired and rent their farms to younger men. Other owners include widows of farmers, business and professional men in small towns, and housewives. While some farm land is owned by relatively large absentee corporate or other owners, in total this area is relatively small. Farm land ownership in the United States is widely distributed.

In spite of some notable instances of large-scale farm land ownership, in general farm land in the United States is widely owned and always has been. The ownership of farm land is closely related to its use and management. This is obviously so for the owner-operator; but many landlords are related to their tenants and are closely involved in the management of the farm. The closeness of the relation between farm land ownership and use is the more remarkable in that farm land in the United States is no longer basic to economic opportunity and to economic security. These have been achieved in other ways—by widespread non-farm employment, by Social Security for protection in old age, and in other ways. Farm land in the United States is more in the hands of those who till it than is true in most nations of the world, and this in spite of the fact that farm land ownership here is less critical to the well-being of people than in most other countries.

FORESTS

Of the nearly 500 million acres of commercial forest land in the United States, slightly more than a fourth is publicly owned, by federal, state, and local governments; and a third is within farms. These we have discussed in the preceding sections of this chapter. This leaves about 40 per cent of the total forest area in other kinds of ownership. About a third of the latter is owned by some kind of forest industry—lumber company, pulp company, or other. Almost all of this is in ownerships of 5,000 acres or more, and two thirds of it is in ownerships of 50,000 acres or more. There are only a comparatively few such forest industry owners—less than 25,000 in the whole nation. They own the most productive private forests, and they have kept their forests in productive condition, for the most part.

In sharp contrast are over a million owners of forest land not associated with a forest industry operation. Nearly two thirds of their holdings are in units of less than 500 acres, and a third are in units of less than 100 acres. Much of this forest is inherently of low productivity, and most of it has been cut and otherwise so managed as to reduce its current productivity still lower. In considering forest land ownership statistics, one should realize that forests are generally far less productive per acre than is farm land; while there are great variations within each, on the average forest land produces about one sixth as much as does farm land. Thus a forest of 500 acres is very small, and one of 5,000 acres may be too small for full-time economic operation by its owner.

This large area and vast number of small private forests not connected with farms is not a productive economic enterprise, and individually they cannot be made so. The same is also true of the larger area and larger number of farm forests. Yet these small, usually low-grade forests do produce some forest product output over a long period of years. Left alone, they will grow some trees which can be harvested for lumber or for pulp; the harvesting usually is profitable. This kind of periodic harvesting of the untended output of nature is not unlike the occasional berry picking that native peoples have done in many parts of the world. It surely is not purposeful production, yet it may yield an appreciable amount of product. Since the economic returns from such small poor forests is so low, we may assume that they are owned primarily for other reasons—for recreation, as a hedge against inflation, for sentimental personal reasons, or for other unknown purposes.

CITIES

We know comparatively little about the ownership of the two thirds of the cities which are privately owned. By far the greater part of the privately owned urban area is used for residential purposes, and most of this is used for single family dwellings with attached yards. Most of this property is owned by its occupiers. Government programs of the past thirty years have enormously stimulated private home ownership. Homes can be bought with small down payments, the monthly payments are often no larger than rent of similar quarters would be, the lender is protected by a system of insured mortgages, and the buyer gets a significant subsidy in being permitted to deduct interest payments from income in calculating income taxes. Some houses, and far more apartments, are occupied by renters. The area of land involved in such rental property may be smaller, but its value is relatively large. While some firms own considerable numbers of apartments, yet in total the ownership of residential property for rent is not highly concentrated.

The ownership of industrial and commercial property is more concentrated than that of residential property, reflecting in large part the larger size of typical business firms. Some businesses own relatively large urban tracts; many small business firms rent all the land or space they need. But land and space is freely available to any person or firm with the money to rent or buy it. As in the case of farm property, the ownership of land in the city is not necessary to economic opportunity or to economic security; in the United States, we have met these needs in other ways.

CHAPTER 11

A Few Sharp Contrasts with Latin America

Colonization of the New World south of the Rio Grande was almost wholly by Spain; the other European countries left little mark here. There are several major contrasts in present land use and land ownership between the North America that was predominantly under British influence during colonization and the Latin America that was under predominantly Spanish influence. While many factors have been operative, the effect of the early colonization is greater than most people realize.

Spanish exploration and early colonization of the New World took place roughly a century earlier than the English and other European exploration and colonization of North America; much of the former was in the sixteenth century, while the latter was mostly in the seventeenth century. At the same time, at any given date Spain was less advanced in its social concepts than was England. Feudalism in Spain during its colonization period was greatly stronger than was feudalism in Britain during its colonization period. Explorers and early colonizers from Spain were frequently adventurers, not too well established within the social and economic structure of the home country; but they were more eager to establish feudalism—a feudalism for their benefit—in the new country than they were motivated to try to change the social order they left at home. Their motives for settlement in the New World

102

were considerably different than were the motives of the later English colonizers, and their methods reflected their motives.

In retrospect, today we may say that Spain was unlucky to have found gold in the New World, although at the time the judgment everywhere would have been that it was very lucky. In fact the early Spanish explorers and colonizers found enormous quantities of gold, by the standards of wealth of the day. They stole it without hesitation from the native peoples who had mined it, and transported it back to the homeland; and the English—and others—tried, often with success, to steal it from the Spaniards en route. The value of the gold obtained in Mexico, Peru, and elsewhere confirmed, for the short run, the wisdom of seeking gold in the new land. But the finding of gold reduced the importance of agriculture and other productive activity in the colonies, which the settlers in North America perforce had turned to. In the end, the large flow of gold into Spain largely ruined that country, by continued inflation and by discouragement to industry and other productive development, and it surely retarded the development of the colonies as well.

SPANISH COLONIZATION

Spanish colonization typically took a very different form from the dominant form of colonization within what is now the United States. There were many variations of each, and what follows describes the typical Spanish form and contrasts it with the typical English form; one could find instances quite different from these typical situations, and possibly even reverse situations.

The Spanish explorers typically obtained grants for themselves and their chief henchmen; these grants were from the king of Spain. Interestingly enough, the first grants were as often for tribes or groups of Indians as they were for land, but grants for land either followed or were made initially. The grants usually covered large acreages of land, and explicitly or implicitly considerable numbers of Indians as well. The grantee assumed certain responsibilities for the latter, but he was permitted and expected to use them in economic production for his benefit. There grew up a system of local lords, chief henchmen, and peons, the latter often slaves for all practical purposes. Interbreeding, as well as sometimes intermarriage, with the Indians took place, creating a new mixed race which was often socially apart from either of its ancestor groups. The grants thus obtained and organized generally became self-sufficient baronies, resembling those of Britain and Europe of a few hundred years earlier. Agriculture was the chief occupation; food and other necessities were produced for the population of the grant, with little imported and little exported from each grant. Transportation was poor, and the various estates lived in a large degree of isolation. While these same characteristics existed for southern plantations in the United States during the colonial period, apparently they were more marked in most of Latin America, and persisted far longer—in fact, to a degree they persist to the present.

Under this system of Spanish colonization, land surveys were sometimes lacking entirely or were very poor when made at all. Such surveys as were made covered only the granted lands, not the total area. Land records were typically poor, and they were not maintained in a central public place. During most of the colonization period, there was no means by which a person could obtain land except by this rather cumbersome royal grant route; the cards were effectively stacked against the type of independent frontier settler of the North American type, but it is also true that there were few or none of the latter.

The Roman Catholic church played a major role in this colonization process also. Spain was and is a Roman Catholic country. The early explorers and colonizers were typically accompanied by priests whose concern was to save the souls of the natives, by converting them to Christianity. Whatever may be our judgment today as to the role of the church in that period, we must admire the courage and devotion of many of these priests. The church accepted the land settlement and colonization practices, including the virtual enslavement of the Indians. These practices conformed to the social standards of the day, and the church was a part of those social standards also. The church itself owned land in many Latin American countries, and had its colonies of converted Indians, who operated church property under generally similar conditions to those found on private holdings. The church was a major conservative instrument, opposing reforms of all kinds; it was supported by, and in harmony with, the large landowners and the type of society they represented. Much later, in some Latin American countries, as Mexico for example, revolts were as much against the church as against the current rulers, and successful revolt often led to sharp curbing of the role of the church.

LAND TITLES IN LATIN AMERICA TODAY

In Latin America today, land titles are frequently defective. All Latin American countries lack comprehensive accurate surveys, which have boundaries clearly defined and marked on the land itself, and which are generally known and accepted by everyone. We have such surveys in the United States, in spite of the lack of perfection in them, and they are basic to our whole system of private property in land. In Latin American countries, land records are also typically poor; and these too are basic to private property

105

in land. In Latin American countries there is a vast amount of land squatting; much land is occupied by someone who does not own it. Not having secure title to it, the squatter cannot improve it or use it as he would if he had such title; and faced with de facto occupancy by another, the nominal owner is prevented from making good use of the land, even if he desired to do so and had the necessary means. In most countries, various laws have been enacted which give the squatter some protection against being dispossessed, but which still do not give him clear possession. The landowner must usually institute lengthy and expensive lawsuits to clear his land under these circumstances.

As a result of these conditions, land in Latin American countries is not freely traded, and often it is difficult as well as expensive to obtain land for any new enterprise, whether urban or rural. Land is generally not mortgaged as security for loans, being not acceptable to lenders because of these circumstances, and in the absence of precedent there is often no legal procedure whereby it could be so pledged, or foreclosed upon if the loan defaulted.

In Latin America today, the land title situation described above, which traces directly to its colonial history, is a serious obstacle to economic development. Until land surveys are made, land records are improved, and legal procedures are clarified and strengthened, deficient land titles will continue to be a major obstacle to economic development in these countries.

LATIFUNDIA AND MINIFUNDIA

Much of Latin America today is held in large estates, often called latifundia, hacienda, or by some other term. In many countries, a very small fraction of all landowners owns far more than half of all the land; moreover, these few large landowners are likely to have the potentially most

106

productive lands of the country. Many of the landowners do not reside on their estates throughout the year, or even at any time. Some are nonresidents of the country. Some, especially in Central American countries, are United States corporations; but the greater number are citizens of the respective countries. The land is worked by tenants or wage workers, who are often literally peons. Those who work for wages often are paid partly in kind and partly in cash. In general, for these people sharecropping is a step upward on the land tenure ladder; we may regard sharecropping as a very primitive form of land tenure, and it has in fact been so in the United States, but for many people in the world it would be an improvement over their present condition. Living conditions for these workers may be poor, yet typically they and their ancestors have lived on the same estate for many generations, and their ties to the land are far more than economic.

The land within these large estates is often not used as fully or as intensively as its physical and economic potentials warrant. Many owners seem to lack economic motivation to strive for maximum income; others lack managerial skill or capital necessary to develop their estates for new kinds of more intensive production. Many such estates continue to emphasize an extensive system of livestock production, which may once have been the most economic use of the land; but more intensive methods and new crops might now produce more output and more net income.

At the same time that these very large estates exist in most Latin American countries, there exist also large numbers of minifundia, or very small farms—too small ever to be good economic units. The man who sought land for his own frequently was forced to get it on the poorer lands of the country, often in the mountains or hilly areas, where the soils are relatively unproductive and subject to severe erosion. Some very destructive land uses are practiced under these conditions. The small tracts of unproductive land yield only a bare subsistence for their owners or operators, which often must be supplemented by wages from work elsewhere. Although living conditions for these small farmers are often very bad, yet they may be better than as peons on the larger estates. The long-run income prospects on these very small farms are poor. Their land area is too small, and their land quality too low; in many cases they represent only a desperation attempt at economic independence under basically unsuitable conditions.

Latin American countries typically lack significant numbers of intermediate-size farms. The large family-size farm, adequate to fully employ one or two men using modern farm machinery but capable of being operated by them, and capable of producing a decent income for all the workers on the farm, is notably lacking in most Latin American countries.

LAND REFORM

As a result of the above situation, land reform is a burning political, economic, and social issue in most Latin American countries today. The demands for land reform cannot be understood if one views it as solely an economic move, or as solely a political issue, or as solely a social movement; it is all three combined. Reformers want better economic opportunity for the masses in each country, and they correctly point out that economic progress in general is impeded by the existing land ownership and use pattern. But their advocacy of land reform goes far deeper than this. The present pattern of land ownership is basic to the whole social structure, to the social order which ranges from lord to peon. It is basic also to the whole political structure, with political power concentrated far more in the hands of the landowners than their numbers alone would justify. In many countries, at least until comparatively recently, government was wholly in the hands of the large landowners. A gradual evolution of society, of political structure, and of the economy is very difficult with a rigid powerful present structure built upon the pattern of land ownership.

Faced with this situation, there are some who would like to destroy the present pattern, no matter what the consequences. The Communists and some who sympathize with them fall into this group. They would accept a severe drop in economic output, if this were necessary, as part of land reform; they would seek the social and political changes that could well come from economic chaos. Land reform need not, of course, mean reduced agricultural output, but it can easily have this result if brought about by violence or by drastic upheaval and destruction of presently established production and marketing mechanisms. To those who find the present situation both galling and a complete block to progress, any change seems better than the present.

In all the Latin American countries there are other groups who seek land reform and change, but who want it to be orderly, rapid, and progressive from the present condition to improved conditions. They want a larger agricultural output, with higher incomes for those who work the soil; they want a less severely structured society, with greater social mobility based more upon personal abilities and less upon inherited position. They want also wider real participation in the political process. But they seek all these changes by legal and gradual means, hoping to avoid severe dislocations while at the same time obtaining significant progress.

In all the countries there are also conservative landowning groups, opposed to change generally and opposed to loss of their special positions in particular. Such groups seek to prevent any of the economic, social, and political changes associated with land reform, or to retard and modify any changes that they cannot prevent. With these major groups, and many variants of each, all seeking to use all economic, social, and political power they possess for their own ends, tensions naturally build up within each country. This is the situation which has arisen in almost every Latin American

	United States	Latin American Countries
Land surveys	Mostly accurate; marked on ground	Usually lacking
Basic land records	Good, on the whole	Frequently defective
Land titles	Secure; enforceable in court	Often seriously be-clouded
Land as a basis for credit	Commonly used	Rarely used; financial and legal institutions lacking
Distribution of farm land ownership	Widely distributed; most farmers own all or part of land they farm	Very unequally distributed; a few very large owners, many very small ones, with only a few middle-sized ones
National attitude toward their own land ownership situation	Mostly satisfied	Widespread dissatisfaction and criticism; land reform a burning national issue

Fig. 21.—Generalized Contrast of Land Situations in the United States and in Many Latin American Countries

country, which has been fully solved in none as yet. It is explosive and dramatic; its solution is not evident as yet. It seems inconceivable that some type of land reform will not occur within the next few decades, but it is far from clear how this reform will be brought about or what the end result will be.

The United States throughout its history has largely or

wholly escaped all of this problem which so dominates Latin America today. The differences between our country and theirs traces directly back to the difference in our respective colonial histories. We are indeed fortunate in the kind of land ownership, land use, and land survey and land record system we have built up; but we cannot in honesty claim that as a nation we deserve the credit. The basic decisions were made in our earlier colonial period, and we have but carried to a logical conclusion those earlier decisions.

CHAPTER 12

Public Land Management Today

In Chapter 9 we related how permanent reservation of land for public use arose; in Chapter 10 we briefly discussed the role of public lands in the total present land ownership situation. In this chapter we shall discuss how the public lands are used and managed.

As we have noted, public lands may be owned by the federal, state, county, or municipal governments. In this chapter we shall focus on the federal lands for two reasons: their area is much greater than that of all other public lands combined, and we have much better information about their use and management than we have for other public lands. While there are some differences, yet other public lands tend to be used and managed in similar ways.

A FEW FACTS ABOUT THE FEDERAL LANDS

As we noted in Chapter 10, over a third of all federal lands today are in Alaska, and half lies in the Rocky Mountains and to their westward. This preponderance of federal land ownership in these states reflects in part their later settlement, for the idea of permanent federal reservations did not take hold until virtually all land had been alienated from public ownership in the Midwest, East and South; and it reflects partly the fact that much of the land in these states is unsuited to agriculture. Nearly all the federal land in these regions has been reserved from original public domain. The lesser acreages elsewhere in the United States have been mostly purchased by the federal government or, as in the case of some national park areas, donated to it by individuals.

A great deal of the present federal land area consists of mountains, deserts, tundra, and similar lands unproductive for agriculture, and often of low productivity for any use. The vast mountain chain of the Rockies and the Cascade-Sierra Nevada, as well as lesser mountain groups, are largely federal in ownership. The deserts of the Great Basin and of western Arizona-southeastern California are nearly wholly federally owned. The vast reaches of Alaska are either tundra or sparse forest, for the most part. The climate of the federal lands varies greatly, but much is arid and semi-arid; the higher elevations in the 48 contiguous states and much of Alaska have short growing seasons and often are very cold much of the year. A great deal of it is above tree-line, being too cold or too windy for trees to grow. All in all the federal land is not the most productive real estate our nation has to offer, at least for agricultural purposes, although some produce forests well.

This physical character of the federal lands is a natural outgrowth of their history. The land disposal process was always a selective one. Settlers and speculators naturally chose the best lands open to them. Their definition of "best" depended upon the circumstances of the day, including technology for using land and transportation facilities for getting to it and from it to market. Mistakes in land selection were made, of course. But by and large the best land available at any particular period was chosen by private land selectors, leaving always in federal ownership the poorest land of that time. This selective process worked not only regionally—the Midwest as against the Far West, for instance—but it also worked within each local area. Land with more gentle topography, better soils, readily

113

available water, or other desirable characteristics was chosen before land lacking these characteristics. When one looks at the land ownership map of a local area and sees scattered public lands intermingled with predominantly private land, one knows without visiting the area that the small federal tracts will be the steeper, rockier, drier, least attractive lands of the whole area in nearly all cases.

This selective land disposal process has led to one other serious result, as far as federal land management is concerned. The intermingling of private and public lands, especially where the land has low productivity and hence must be managed in large blocks, seriously affects public land management. Not only must the private owners be given access to their lands, however inconvenient this may be, but often they are in a position to use the federal lands, either with or without authority to do so, much more readily than can any other possible private landowner. A preferred position therefore accrues to these people, regardless of the intent of the federal land managing agencies. The extent of intermingled private land ownership varies greatly according to the type of federal area. For national parks, it is about 4 per cent; for national forests, about a fifth; and for grazing districts, about two fifths. The man who owns a ranch within a national park has a magnificent dude ranch, largely of public lands, for instance.

USES OF FEDERAL LANDS

Outdoor recreation is the use of federal lands which affects the largest number of people. In 1960, total visits to the national park system were 79 million, to the national forests 93 million, to federal wildlife refuges 11 million, with lesser numbers to other federal areas. These are *visits*, not persons; they are comparable to movie or other admissions. Since the total visits to even these federal areas is about the same as the total number of people in the United States, and since we know from general observation that many people were unable to visit such areas, it is obvious that some people went two, three, or more times during the year. This is especially clear when one considers that in the same year visits to reservoirs built by the Corps of Engineers totaled 120 million, visits to TVA reservoirs were 53 million, and visits to state parks were 258 million. We do not know how many different individuals may be represented by these total admissions. Considering that some people are too young or too old, ill or infirm, located inconveniently for any of these areas, cannot afford even modest costs for visiting them, or just plain are uninterested in outdoor recreation, it is probable that not much more than half of the total population enjoyed these various areas.

People go to the federal land areas for many different kinds of outdoor recreation. Some are interested primarily in sightseeing, perhaps not even leaving their cars for this purpose; others engage in quiet forest enjoyment, or picnic, or swim, or camp overnight. Some engage in fishing, fewer in hunting; and a few strenuous souls climb mountains, explore caves, or otherwise enjoy the particular qualities of the more rugged outdoors.

The trend has been steeply and regularly upward in these outdoor recreation activities. In general, each year total use is about 10 per cent more than in the preceding year; and this upward trend has been evident for many, many years. Moreover, it continues at the same percentage rate even as total use mounts to higher and higher levels. The basic factors behind the steadily growing use have been more people, higher real incomes per person, more leisure, and better transportation facilities.

Grazing by domestic livestock is another important use of federal lands. A substantial proportion of all ranchers in the localities where there are extensive federal lands graze their livestock at some season on such lands. Although the total amount of forage so obtained is rather small, this use of federal land is often strategic because it takes place at a particular season. The privately owned lands usually provide harvested crops for winter feed, and often spring and fall grazing also; national forests are primarily summer grazing areas. Grazing districts provide forage at different seasons, but usually not to the same livestockman; that is, a rancher may obtain winter grazing on the desert for his sheep, or spring-fall grazing for either cattle or sheep, or in some cases summer grazing for either class of livestock, but rarely for all three, or even for two, seasons. Intricate patterns of private and public land use have arisen because of these seasonal factors. Grazing use of national forests has been declining for many years and has been about stable on the grazing districts.

Timber harvest is another important use of some federal lands, especially the national forests and the O & C lands to which we referred in Chapter 9. In an earlier day, when there was ample mature timber on privately owned land, usually more accessible to markets than are the federal areas, the demand for the federal timber was relatively low. However, as the private forest lands increasingly were harvested, their remaining area was bought up by the large private timber processors. The smaller processors, and any others who did not acquire their own forest land, were increasingly dependent upon purchase of federal timber. Today only a fifth of all forest land is federally owned, although in the West where federal ownership is heaviest, three fifths is so owned; but the federal lands support over 40 per cent of all mature timber. During the Second World War and since, the private timber-processing industry substantially expanded its capacity until today there is more capacity than is needed to supply the market, or than the raw material supply will support on a sustained yield basis. When federal timber is offered for sale, competition to buy it is often intense, and processors often bid prices up to levels which leave them little or no profit.

Total volume of timber sold from federal lands has climbed rapidly in recent years. Before the war, about 2 billion board feet were cut annually from national forests; today, the annual cut is roughly 9 billion board feet. The cut from O & C and public domain lands has climbed upward more modestly and is on a much lower level, in the general neighborhood of 1 billion board feet. These great increases in timber harvest have taken place within the sustained yield capacity of the lands; as mature forests are cut, new growth is possible on the cutover lands, which can in turn be harvested in fifty to one hundred years, when the presently mature forests have mostly all been cut. In fact, by various methods of intensive forest management, the sustained yield capacity of federal forest lands could be increased considerably, to somewhere in the 15 to 20 billion board foot annual harvest range.

Dramatic changes have taken place in the price at which timber is sold from federal lands, especially in the years immediately following the war. Before and during the war (the latter under the influence of wartime price controls), the price of standing trees, or stumpage, seldom exceeded $4 per thousand board feet for all timber sold from federal lands; by 1956, the average price of timber sold from national forests was $14, and from O & C lands (with their more valuable old-growth Douglas fir), the average was $38. These price rises for federal timber had their counterpart on private lands; they reflect primarily the scarcity of remaining old-growth timber in private ownership, and the buying up by the larger timber processors of that which does remain.

Federal lands are also leased for private exploration for economically exploitable minerals, especially oil and gas. Most such leases are "wildcat"; the lessee hopes that he, or someone else, will drill for oil and gas, but much leased land is never drilled and much that is drilled does not yield oil. However, substantial revenues are obtained from these leases, partly from relatively small annual rentals on non-producing leases but primarily from royalties (usually one eighth the value of output) from the producing leases. Federal lands are also leased for coal, potash, sodium, and other mineral development. In addition, private persons may obtain title to the land for other mineral development, such as gold, silver, lead, copper, uranium, and other metals.

Federally owned lands are also highly important for watershed purposes. A substantial proportion of all stream flow in the West originates on national forests. The grazing lands at lower elevation often contribute heavily to the sediment load in streams. Many municipalities get their water supply from federally owned watersheds. Protection of these and other watersheds from fire and erosion is a highly important purpose of federal land management.

GOVERNMENT PROCESSES FOR FEDERAL LAND MANAGEMENT

The general public obtains use of the federal lands and their products under a wide variety of arrangements. Anyone is free to use any public recreation area, sometimes with payment of a small fee, often without charge; and for most federal areas one may also use other areas than those designated for recreation, if one observes simple rules and precautions about fire and other hazards. Most timber is sold at competitive sale; prospective purchasers are required to bid against each other, and the timber is awarded to the highest bidder. Mineral leases on proven productive areas are sold the same way. Most mineral leases are non-competitive, however, and the first applicant is awarded the lease. Grazing permits and leases are not sold competitively; applicants are ordinarily required to own property on which the livestock can be cared for during the rest of the year when not on federal land. In practice, grazing leases tend to remain in the same hands or for the

Life cycle of a budget

Year 1: Starts in spring, with a "ceiling" request and authorization

In fall, detailed review by Bureau of Budget

December or January, in President's official budget

Winter and spring, Congressional Committee review, and ultimate action by the Congress

President signs

Year 2: Funds committed or obligated, for various purposes authorized in appropriation act

Part of funds spent, as contracts fulfilled

Year 3: Rest of funds spent, all obligations liquidated

Weaknesses

Investment of capital treated like current expenditures, contrary to recognized business practice

Wealth-yielding appropriations treated like ordinary government expenditures

Little or no consideration to most profitable level of expenditures

Too slow to respond to new economic or social conditions

Budgets made up too far in advance of time to which they apply

Whole process tends to be inflexible, responds too slowly to meet emergencies

Strengths

An open public review of public business

A positive control over activities of public agencies

An organized, established procedure

Fig. 22.—Budgeting-Appropriation-Expenditure Process of the Federal Government as Applied to Land Management

same private properties for long periods of time. The many miscellaneous uses of federal land take place under a wide variety of arrangements.

The federal land managing agencies each have a central office in Washington; each has regional or state offices, or both; and each has local offices, on or near the land actually managed, readily accessible locally to the using public. Because the federal lands are spread over such a wide area, and because natural and economic conditions vary so greatly within that area, the federal agencies have been forced to give their local representatives broad discretionary authority to deal with situations as they arise. Rules and regulations have been drawn up, and modified over the years, and are published; these govern private use of such lands, and the federal employees follow such rules and regulations in their day-to-day actions and decisions. The federal land managing personnel are almost all technically trained in a university; they are recruited and serve under a Civil Service system which largely removes them from political pressures.

Funds for management of the federal lands are obtained by an intricate and lengthy budgeting-appropriation-expenditure process. In most agencies estimates of manpower and other requirements for proper land management originate at the local office level and are summarized, perhaps modified, at regional and national offices. A budget request is made, reviewed by the Bureau of the Budget, and finally approved by the President; it may, of course, undergo modification in this process. Then it goes to the Congress, which may grant all the money requested, but often makes reductions, and sometimes increases funds for special purposes. The requests are not merely for one big total; their purpose is carefully spelled out, and the final appropriation often sets limits to the use of money for particular purposes. Once the funds are obtained, their actual expenditure must follow established legal procedures and is subject to review by the General Accounting Office, which is an arm of the Congress, to insure that money is honestly and competently spent. This whole process involves many technical details, many men and women, and much time; while it has some special features because it is public business, any private organization of the same size would also have a complex financial process—possibly an even more complex one.

One weakness of this budget-appropriation-expenditure process for federal agencies is the way investment decisions are handled. Funds for investment are treated in the same way as funds for current operation. This practice was long ago abandoned by private business. Money spent to build a road this year produces benefits for many years into the future, as does money spent this year to equip a factory. It is unreasonable to charge all these expenditures against this year's business. On the other hand, money spent last year and in earlier years, for investment purposes, properly should have a charge for depreciation this year, next year, and until the facility is worn out or written off the books. Federal investments would be more profitable if they were handled under the same principles as are private investments, including the establishment of a capital account; and if they were made when the prospects are good for their being profitable, even when this may make a temporary cash deficit.

Products and uses of federal land are priced to the users under a wide variety of arrangements. As we have noted, timber is sold competitively, and so are a few mineral leases. With these exceptions, all uses of federal lands are on terms more favorable than would be available from private landowners. Grazing fees are much lower than rentals of private grazing land, even when allowance is made for the substantial differences in productivity because of the selective process of land disposal discussed above; noncompetitive mineral leases are often at a lower rental than is paid for private lands in the same localities; and recreation use is free or nearly so. Many of the more difficult land management problems of federal agencies arise out of these prices that are below a competitive market level. A private businessman, faced with expensive and difficult demands in excess of his capacity to supply them, would ordinarily raise his prices to a level that offered him some prospect of profit. Federal agencies are restrained from doing this, by law, custom, or their own caution. Low prices or free use undoubtedly encourage more use, and sometimes more careless and destructive use, than would otherwise take place.

THE ROLE OF THE PROFESSIONAL LAND MANAGER

Although the Congress makes the laws and the President decides major issues of policy, in point of fact the management of the federal lands is dominantly in the hands of professional land managers. As the federal lands become more intensively used, the problems of their best administration become more complex. Skill and courage were needed to control forest fires in the early days, for instance, but the management of recreation or timber or grazing resources today calls for much more technical knowledge. Most of the men in the federal agencies are college trained, and most are career men who look forward to a professional life spent in one agency or in similar jobs in other agencies. In college and elsewhere, they are taught high standards of public service. Whereas at one time a forester could be reasonably well informed on all aspects of forest management, today's problems are so complex that some are likely to specialize in forest diseases, others in the control of forest insects, others in silviculture, others in forest engineering, and so on through a long line of forestry specialties.

One reason that the public employee must be well informed if he is to be a good land manager is that the user-public is becoming well informed also. If the agency forester estimates that there are 20 million board feet of commercially harvestable timber on a particular sale, forest industry

I. NEED FOR PROFESSIONAL EXPERTISE IS INCREASING

   Land management problems are growing more complex

   Increased intensity of land use magnifies management problems

   User public is growing more informed

II. PROFESSIONAL LAND MANAGERS ARE BECOMING MORE ENTRENCHED IN AGENCIES

   Minimum professional qualifications generally required

   Civil service, merit system, procedures increasingly used

   Political considerations declining except for key spots

III. TRAINING OF PROFESSIONAL LAND MANAGERS

   Becoming increasingly important

   Usually in physical sciences such as forestry and range management

   Men often imbued with spirit of public service

   Training often lacks basic social sciences

IV. PROFESSIONAL LAND MANAGERS AND POLITICAL PRESSURES

   Increasing use of public lands results in greater but more diffused political pressures

   Interest groups often have opposing interests and pressures

   Professional land manager increasingly plays one pressure group against others

   Professional land managers often get into situations where their basic training provides no guidelines

FIG. 23.—ROLE OF PROFESSIONAL LAND MANAGERS

foresters are likely to be able to correct him if he is wrong. Or if the public agency employee estimates that a particular range will provide forage for only twenty cows, ranchers will be quick to argue with him if they think it can provide more forage than this. And so on, with each major land use.

As the demand for use of federal lands increase, the professional land manager must increasingly try to reconcile one use with another, and sometimes to choose among possible uses. This requires technical knowledge on his part, as to the degree to which different uses are actually in conflict. It also requires ability to get along with people, in order to get different groups to see the interests and problems of the rival groups. In the end, the professional manager may have to refuse one use in order to permit another, and this necessarily requires that he evaluate each use in terms of values which he considers important.

Although increasing use of the federal lands places new responsibilities on the professional land manager, it also offers him many opportunities. When there is only one dominant user group, and possibly only a few dominant individuals within that group, the professional land manager must pit his knowledge and his ideas of public benefits against the demands of that group. When there are several groups, each demanding what it wants, but with mutually incompatible requests, then some compromise is obviously necessary. Under these circumstances, the technical knowledge of the professional land manager may well be decisive. No group can effectively use political pressures under these circumstances, for the other interest groups probably have more or less offsetting political power. The professional land manager who is exposed to more demands and pressures is, paradoxically, freed to a large degree of any single pressure.

As nearly all kinds of use of federal lands continue to increase, the professional land manager will almost certainly grow in importance. Day-to-day administrative issues will be settled by such men, and to an increasing extent policy decisions will be based upon their judgment and upon their knowledge of facts. This makes more important than ever the dedication of these men to the public service.

THE IMPORTANCE OF THE PUBLIC
AS USER

By all odds the most important single factor in federal land management is the use which the public seeks to make of these lands. Fifty years ago or more, when many kinds of use were of small extent, the kind of public land management had to be adapted to that level of public demand. The professional forester might feel that certain forested areas should be harvested, but if there was no market for the logs, he was helpless to carry out the management plans he would choose. Or if the demand for logs were weak he might be able to sell them, but not if he required the logger to carry out good forestry practices in the harvest. If there were few recreationists, there was little need to establish campgrounds or other special facilities to serve them. Many other examples could be cited, showing how the management of federal lands was affected by the level of demand for them.

On the other hand, when demand is high and is mounting each year, as is the case with outdoor recreation in many areas today, the public land manager must cope with this high demand. He cannot refuse to accept recreationists unless he is prepared to take the drastic step of closing roads to visitors; instead, he must somehow provide for them. Their numbers and the activities they seek will go far to determine the manpower and expenditures necessary to manage the area properly. With a demonstrated high demand, he can usually persuade the appropriating authorities to provide enough funds to meet the demand. When the demand is high for timber to buy, he must inventory the available timber supply, determine how much can be sold within the sustained yield principle, lay out reasonable and efficient sale units on which timber buyers

125

will bid and pay the best prices, and supervise the timber harvest operations of the successful bidder. Often he will find it necessary, or at least advantageous, to expend public funds to build roads into forested areas, so that buyers may be charged higher prices for the timber they buy.

In literally a thousand ways the management of public lands is affected by the demands the public makes of those lands. The professional land manager can accommodate those demands in different ways, and he can sometimes influence the use the public seeks; but to a large extent he must operate within the limits set by public demand.

CHAPTER 13

Agricultural Land Use and Tenure

As we pointed out in Chapter 10, more than 80 per cent of the entire 48 contiguous states is in farms; this large area, plus the historic role farming has played in American life, warrants a closer look at farms and farmers. Farms are, strictly speaking, more a kind of business organization than a land use. Included within farms are not only crop and intensive pasture land, but also extensive areas of native grazing lands, large areas of forest, and land used for recreation and other kinds of land uses. Nevertheless, the chief reason for the existence of most farms is to produce agricultural commodities, including commodities used by the farm family as well as those sold.

We have pointed out in several earlier chapters that the United States was once primarily an agricultural nation. During the formative colonial and early national period, most people lived on farms and made most or all of their living there. Many of our political and social institutions owe their origin to the farming era of national history, or still bear many traces of that early history. The traditional school year, with the summer vacation, originated at a time when boys and girls were expected to work on the farm during the summer but were able to go to school in the winter, when farm work was less pressing.

Although agriculture is the traditional form of American life and economy, yet present-day agriculture is one of the most dynamic and changing aspects of our culture and economy. Some historians make much of the Industrial

Revolution, the second half of the eighteenth century and the first half of the nineteenth, when the pace of industrial change was much greater than anything previously known. By comparison, the present-day agricultural revolution is much more dynamic. During the past two decades, the pace of agricultural development in the United States has been much more rapid than has been the pace of industrial development. In this chapter we shall briefly present some information about the kind and speed of the changes under way in agriculture.

PRESENT AGRICULTURAL LAND USE

Of the 1,150 million acres (more or less) in farms in the 48 contiguous states, about 400 million acres are in crops (including fallow crop land, crop failure, etc.), about 525 million acres are in pasture of varying degrees of improvement and productivity, and about 200 million acres are in forest. Of the crop land, more than half is used to raise hay and other forage crops, and for feed grains to support livestock. On an acreage basis, therefore, farm land use in the United States is overwhelmingly oriented toward livestock production. Several factors are responsible for this heavy emphasis upon livestock. Nearly everyone in the United States eats meat; vegetarians are numerically not important. Although meat is, in some respects, a luxury food, yet our average incomes are high enough to allow us to be a relatively heavy meat-eating nation, by world standards. If we were largely vegetarian, or if incomes were too low to support large meat purchases, we could as a nation shift very largely toward eating grains and other crop products, with the result that we could feed several times as many people from the present crop acreage. China, India, and other nations are forced to do just this. Another measure of our relative well-being is that we use for livestock pasture land which in poorer nations would be used to produce crops for human consumption; its per acre yield would be relatively low, but it would still support more people than when used to produce meat.

We use slightly more than 50 million acres of crop land to produce food grains, chiefly wheat. We have used much more than this, at times past, when the need for wheat was greater, as during wartime. Even so, we produce more than twice as much wheat as we eat, as a nation; the rest is sold abroad. We have experienced increasing difficulty selling this surplus wheat abroad, even when the price is heavily subsidized by the federal government. As a nation we have the capacity to produce far more wheat than we need. As per capita incomes have risen, and as diets have come to include more fruits and vegetables, our per capita consumption of wheat has fallen off. Wheat, made into bread, is a staple article of diet, but we will not buy more if the price falls or if our incomes rise; and if past trends continue, our children will eat even less bread than we do.

Cotton is an important cash crop, an industrial crop partly for consumption within the country, partly for export. Acreage has varied considerably, but in recent years it has not taken much more than 10 million acres. Once when cotton yields per acre were much lower and when other countries around the world were growing much less cotton than today, our cotton acreage was much larger. We grow various kinds of oil crops—soybeans, peanuts, and others—on a larger acreage, close to 30 million acres annually in recent years. Tobacco and sugar beets are two highly specialized crops that take relatively small acreages but use a great deal of labor and produce a highly valued crop.

Although the acreage of fruits and vegetables of all kinds totals to only about 10 million acres annually—about the same as cotton today—yet the farm value of these varied crops is greater than that of all the hay and forage crops, which occupy about eight times the area. These specialized crops often occupy land of special qualities, such as long growing season and freedom from frost. Like tobacco, they require a great deal of labor but produce a high gross income per acre.

There is a high degree of regional specialization in crop and livestock production. One major factor is climate; some crops cannot be grown at all in certain parts of the United States; others yield much better in some areas than elsewhere. Economic advantage, including proximity to market, is often important. Sometimes it is the way different crops fit together into a farm operation which is most important. In order to take advantage of extensive pasture acreages, some forage crops for winter feeding of livestock may be necessary, for instance. Some farms are highly specialized. For instance, many farms produce only wheat. Others have one major crop or kind of livestock but may have some less important types of production also. Still others have several crops or kinds of livestock, fitted together in an intricate and diversified pattern. American agriculture exhibits great geographical and organizational diversity, as one would expect from such a large and varied country.

TRENDS IN OUTPUT OF FARM LANDS

American agriculture has changed greatly over the past, especially in the past twenty or thirty years, so that some more detailed consideration of its historical development is essential. Agricultural history in the United States can be divided into two major periods or eras: from 1790 to roughly 1920, and from about 1920 until the present.

From the beginning of the nation until roughly the First World War, the total acreage in farms, the acreage of crop land, the number of farms, the number of work animals on farms, and total agricultural output all expanded, each at about the same regular rate, as nearly as we can tell from the available data. These were the great exploring decades, the settlement period, the period of development of new land which we have to some extent described in earlier chapters. People swept west across the nation, taking land from public ownership into private use and control, clearing forests, plowing forest and prairie alike, building homes, developing farms. It was an agriculture powered by work animals and human muscle. During these long decades, total agricultural output and total consumption of agricultural commodities in the United States rose together, and each paralleled the rise in total population. We exported some commodities throughout, and we imported some; but we consumed most of what we produced and produced most of what we consumed. In the early decades, this statement was true for the individual farms as well; later, farms specialized more, and more of the consumers lived in cities, but as a nation we largely produced for ourselves. These were decades of great change, of the expansionist kind. This was the period when the chief means of increasing food supply was by increasing crop acreage; some people even insisted it was the only way.

Since roughly 1920, or the time of the First World War, sharply divergent trends have developed within agriculture. The acreage of crop land has hardly changed at all, modest decreases in some areas being about balanced by increases elsewhere; the labor force in agriculture has declined by half; animal power has been almost wholly replaced by mechanical power; and total agricultural output has doubled. It is these drastic and divergent trends that lead us and many others to describe these changes as an agricultural revolution. The parallel trends of crop acreage, labor supply, work animals, and output have parted company; some have gone up, others have stayed steady, and others have declined. The key to a doubled output from the same area and with half the labor force is new agricultural technology. Improved varieties, more and cheaper fertilizers, better insect and disease control, greater ability to perform crop operations at the proper season, and other factors have been responsible for the changes.

The agricultural revolution is not over, but will continue for a long time. There is reason to believe that we may be

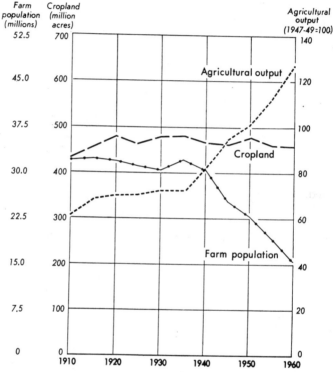

FIG. 24.—TRENDS IN AGRICULTURAL OUTPUT, CROP LAND, AND FARM POPULATION SINCE 1910

The current agricultural revolution in the United States is revealed by this chart. From the same area of crop land, with half as many people on the farm, agricultural output more than doubled in fifty years. These changes are still under way, and further dramatic developments are probable over the next fifty years or less.

on the threshhold of faster and more dramatic changes. Our productive capacity has led to agricultural surpluses over most of the past forty or fifty years; moreover, except in wartime, our agricultural productive capacity has not been stretched to its limit. We could have produced more, had prices and markets warranted it. It seems highly probable that agricultural surpluses will continue for a long time. Agricultural productive capacity will continue to rise, probably faster than will the demand for agricultural commodities. The result is surplus.

There are many forces which lead a farmer to adopt new technology and increase his output, even when the result of all farmers doing this is to lower prices to the point where incomes are no higher, and may be lower, under the new than under the old technology. The amount any one farmer can produce is so small, in comparison with total output, that he properly ignores the effects of his output on prices of the commodities he produces. Many, perhaps most, farms have some surplus labor; if some means can be found to employ it productively, income on that farm will be increased. Most new farm machines and most new farm technology is output-increasing in effect. The farmer who adopts it increases his output, the one who does not fails to increase his output, and each gets the same price on the market. As a result of these and other forces, farmers are under considerable pressure to adopt new technologies, which mean more output in nearly all cases. It is not inconsistent, therefore, to expect increased agricultural output to the point where surpluses are chronic, while at the same time to anticipate relatively low farm incomes.

FARMS AND FARMERS

Reference has been made to the large decline in farm numbers in the past generation; this deserves a more care-

133

ful and detailed look. At the peak, as late as 1935, there were about 6.5 million farms in the United States. Many of these were quite small, as economic enterprises. A tract of three acres or more, producing $250 or more worth of agricultural commodities, was classed as a farm. More than a fourth were self-sufficient farms—i.e., more of their total production was consumed on the farm than was sold from it; or they were part-time farms, enterprises on which the operator spent only part of his time, while working for wages the rest of the time. But nearly another fourth produced less than $2,500 worth of total output, measured in terms of today's prices. Although these small farms had relatively low cash operating costs at that time, yet they obviously could not have large net incomes. With low incomes, living conditions on farms necessarily were poor; most farmers then lacked electricity, modern plumbing, and other health and comfort necessities.

Since 1935 major changes have taken place, not only as to the total number of farms, but equally in other respects. The total number of farms has declined by nearly half, as we have noted, until there are only a few more than 3.5 million today. Most of this decline has taken place because young men have been reluctant to enter farming—hard work and low incomes have naturally frightened them off. Older men die and retire, but there has been little or no accelerated withdrawal of older men from farming. Young men, usually better educated than their fathers, more employable in different occupations, and without deep roots in agriculture, have been more willing to leave for the small towns and cities, and for other occupations. Older men, knowing only farming, with their emotional roots deep in rural living, have been less willing to leave; and many would have encountered employers' prejudices against older workers had they attempted to find new jobs in cities. These changes are natural enough, but in many rural communities they have meant that the farmers are getting preponderantly old, that the age structure is getting distorted, with all that this means for social institutions of all kinds.

At the same time that these markedly divergent trends were arising according to the age of farmers, major changes

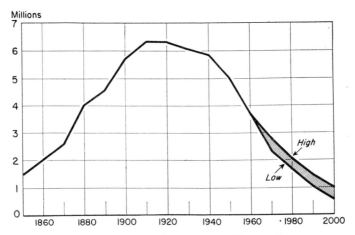

FIG. 25.—NUMBER OF FARMS IN THE UNITED STATES, 1850–1960, AND PROJECTIONS TO 2000

As western settlement moved swiftly forward, the number of farms in the United States more than trebled from 1850 to 1910. Following thirty years of roughly constant numbers, substantial reductions took place, bringing us today back to fewer farms than in 1880. Major further reductions in farm numbers seem inevitable, and by 2000 we probably shall have many fewer farms than in 1850.

were taking place in the economic size of farms. The greatest reduction has been in farms with less than $2,500 gross income, in terms of today's prices; they have declined from 3.5 million in 1935 to 1.5 million in 1959. Farms of the next larger size, those with $2,500 to $5,000 gross income, have also declined in numbers during the same period, but not so drastically. Larger farms have increased in number, the

135

largest sizes the most, comparatively. These changes in farm numbers according to farm size are partly due to some smaller ones actually ceasing to operate and to the establishment of some new larger ones; to some extent, however, the same farmer with the same basic farm unit has found ways of increasing his farm output so as to result in his reclassification in a larger economic size. At the same time, farm operating expenses as a proportion of gross farm income have risen, so that the same gross farm income today may not represent as large a net income as it did twenty years or more ago (this on the basis of the same prices at each period).

The best indications are that future changes in farm numbers and farm size will be a continuation of these trends, at least for the next two decades or longer. Young men will continue to avoid entering farming, while older men will withdraw only as death and retirement normally take them out; the result will be many fewer farmers than at present, but proportionately an older group than now. The adjustments in many rural areas are by no means complete. If farmers are to share in the general growth in real income which characterizes our economy as a whole, they must find ways of increasing both gross and net output per farm. In this modern age, there is little future in a farm which can produce no more than $2,500 gross income—and little more for one that can produce no more than $5,000. Farms with $20,000 gross income once were large; in another generation, they will be average or smaller.

These changes in numbers of farms have been accompanied by considerable changes in farm tenure as well. In 1935, 41 per cent of all farms were operated by tenants; while they averaged smaller than owner-operated farms, yet they included nearly a third of crop acreage. A fourth of the tenants were sharecroppers, who provided only unskilled labor to use machinery, work animals, and land pro-

136

vided by the landlord. About half of the croppers were Ne-groes. But many other tenants were only a little further up the tenure ladder; they may have owned some machinery and livestock, but they too tended to operate small farms for low incomes. On many rented or leased farms the farm income, small as it was, had to support not only the tenant family but often the landlord's family as well.

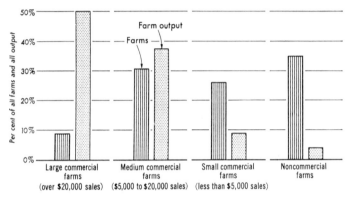

FIG. 26.—FARM OUTPUT BY SIZE OF FARM, 1959

There is enormous variation in the productivity of farms in the United States. At one extreme are the noncommercial farms, a third of the total number but with less than 5 per cent of total output; at the other extreme, less than 10 per cent of the largest farms produce just half of the whole agricultural output. The small commercial farms seem to have no real economic future; their output is so low that no price level can make them profitable.

Today, the situation is considerably different. Croppers as a distinctive group have shrunk to one sixth of their former peak number, and tenants of all kinds are down to one fourth of their peak numbers. Full owners have de-clined somewhat from their 1935 peak, but are still at two thirds of that level. The decline in area of land in full-owner farms has been much less, the present area being only 12 per cent below the peak; even all tenant farms have declined in area only about one half. These smaller declines in farm area than in farm numbers is further evidence of the increasing average size of these farms. One of the greatest changes has taken place in the part-owner class; these are men who own some land and rent some—though called part-owner, they could with equal accuracy be called part-tenant. Their present numbers are actually 21 per cent above their 1935 numbers; more significantly, their present area is nearly double their 1935 area. Renting of land, either temporarily or as a continuing arrangement, has often been a way to increase farm size quickly and with a minimum of capital; hence the great rise in the part-owner as a tenure class.

Changes in numbers and acreage of farms by tenure class may not be the whole story; a farm owner burdened by mortgage debt may in fact be no better off than a tenant. During the First World War land values rose greatly, largely under a stimulus of speculative land buying; and these increased land prices were financed largely by increased mortgage debt. These mortgages were either foreclosed or paid off later, when prices of farm commodities were much lower; they represented a real burden on agriculture through the 1920's. In the 1930's, when the Great Depression struck, land values fell still further and more mortgages were either foreclosed or written down. The level of farm mortgage debt reached about half the value of land and buildings in 1935. In the prosperous years of the Second World War and immediately afterward, a large part of this debt was paid off; having been burned by excessive debt earlier, many farmers, especially the older ones, were anxious to get out of debt. After the war, however, younger farmers seeking to enter agriculture often incurred debts, sometimes relatively large ones. Total mortgage debt began to rise shortly after the war, and it has risen substantially in recent years. Until the late 1950's the ratio of debt to land value fell, because land values went up faster than did debt. In more recent years, however, the ratio of debt has risen again, but it is still not much over a fourth of the value of land and buildings. These average figures, however, conceal many significant differences among farmers. Older prosperous farmers are often out of debt; younger ones who began farming with very limited assets of their own may be in debt to a burdensome degree, with serious doubt of their ability to repay the mortgage in the future. The amount of money required to engage in farming on a scale that promises an adequate income has risen very greatly in the past two decades; yet it is not the size of the capital requirement, but its relation to the annual earning power of the farm which is most significant. If farm incomes are relatively high, a heavy load of debt can be carried and repaid without too much difficulty; if farm incomes are relatively low, even a small mortgage may be too much.

FAMILY FARMS

The idea of the independent farmer, owning the land he farms, living by his own labor, and beholden to no man has long been associated with Thomas Jefferson, who glorified such farmers perhaps more than has any other equally prominent person. This ideal appealed greatly to the American spirit and idealism; for a long time we believed that we had such an agriculture. There was indeed some validity to this dream. The frontier had encouraged independent farm operation, and land had been relatively plentiful. Most farms were relatively small, and they remained so while industry was evolving into relatively large units.

But there were always major exceptions to the dream. The South had had plantations almost from the earliest colonial days, and these were based to a major degree upon slavery—a far cry from the independent farm yeomanry we so admired! But there were large ranches in the West, with their relatively large numbers of hired cowboys. In some localities there were "factory farms," hiring relatively large numbers of seasonal laborers, even from rather early days. The typical family farm often employed one or more hired hands during part or all the year. Much was made of the agricultural ladder: the farmer's son started as hired hand, on his father's farm or on another farm in the community; saved his money until he could rent a farm; operated it as a tenant a few years; and then bought a farm of his own. This picture too had some validity, even though a substantial proportion of the hired workers never got above wage work, and a substantial proportion of the tenants never achieved farm ownership.

In the past twenty years or so, major changes have taken place among tenure groups also, as we have noted. The amount of hired labor per farm has been steadily declining; with better machinery, farm operators can do more of the work themselves. The Negro sharecropper as a distinctive form of tenancy has all but disappeared; it is probable that in most cases this was the landlord's decision, not his. The number of share tenants has declined. An old form of tenancy has assumed much larger proportions: the part-owner, who is also part-tenant. With the great enlargement in farms since the war, many a farm owner was unable to buy the land he wanted, or hesitated to incur the debt that would be necessary, and he chose to rent a farm to add to the one he owned. This form of tenancy now includes nearly a fourth of all farms, and includes a larger acreage than any other tenure group.

All of these facts are evidence that the family farm is changing. It is not weakening; rather it is growing stronger. There is less dependence upon hired labor, more upon operator's labor; fewer farms are substandard, more are adequate family farm units. Those who have strong sentiments favoring family farms need not despair; their future is not threatened, if they can learn to grow and change as times change.

CHAPTER 14

Urban Land Use and Control

We lack a clear and universally accepted definition of "urban land," and this unavoidably makes discussion of the subject more difficult. On the one hand there is some confusion between the city as a legal area, and the city as a form of living and of land use. Some data properly relate to cities as legal areas, but for most purposes our interest is greater in the city as an economic or land use area. Much land properly belonging to the city in the latter sense of the term lies outside the legal city. Another confusion arises as to the extent of the area to include, even under the concept of the economic city. Land which is more or less definitely in use for residential, commercial, industrial, and associated uses obviously belongs in the economic city. But what about idle land in or adjacent to such a city? There are often vacant lots, comparatively small areas sandwiched in between developed areas; larger "leapfrogged" idle areas, bypassed at least for the present in the general development process, but more or less surrounded by developed areas; and then there is always an idle peripheral belt around the economic city, of land hopefully "ripening" for development later, but which has now been taken out of any other use. Do all of these, too, belong to the "city"?

Depending upon the definition one uses, the area of urban land in the United States today may range from as little as 15 million acres, or even less, to as much as 40 million, or even more. In any case, this is not more than 1 to 2 per cent of the total land area of the 48 contiguous states, and

142

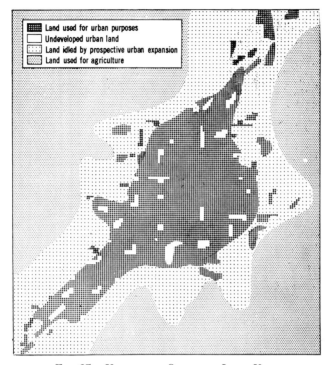

FIG. 27.—URBAN AND SUBURBAN LAND USE

The typical city contains a good deal of idle land; even greater is the area of land idled around its periphery, waiting for later urban expansion. Much land is taken out of agriculture or forestry long before it is needed for urban uses.

thus may not seem important. Yet it is altogether possible that the raw land value of this 1 to 2 per cent is as great as the raw land value of the other 98 or 99 per cent of the total land area. Moreover, at least two thirds of all the people live in cities, more than two thirds of the physical wealth of the nation is located there, and more than two thirds of the national income originates in the city. By any

143

of these tests, urban land is the most important in the whole nation, however small its area.

Urban land acquires its value and has its usefulness as *site*. That is, it represents, above all, a place convenient for working, living, and nearly all the myriad activities of production and consumption in the modern world. The fertility of urban land is a distinctly secondary matter, for instance. Cities may perform many economic functions in production, transportation, trade, government, and the like; but in each case, it is the site qualities which give the urban land its value.

The value of a particular tract of urban land and its improvements depends as much or more upon the activities of neighbors as it does upon the activities of its owner or occupant. No matter how well you maintain your home, for instance, if the neighborhood in which you live is deteriorating, your property will almost certainly be losing its value. On the other hand, even a neglected house in a good neighborhood is likely to hold up in value relatively well. As the land use in a neighborhood changes, you may be forced to change the use of your property also. One can often see an old home in a once good neighborhood that hangs on after stores or factories have invaded the area; but in time its owners will conclude that this is no longer a good residential neighborhood for them either. In the city, much more than in the country, one is affected by the actions of one's neighbors; and your own actions influence other people too.

It is very difficult to separate urban land, as such, from such land with its improvements. In this chapter, although we shall refer only to land, we shall mostly include the improvements also.

144

PUBLIC EFFECTS ON URBAN LAND USE

As we noted in Chapter 10, about one third of the entire urban area of the United States (however defined) is publicly owned. Most of this land consists of streets and alleys, but some is parks, playgrounds, and other public areas. The proportion of public land is higher in small cities and towns than in large ones; the proportionate area of streets, in particular, falls as city size increases. In most cities there is more publicly owned land than there is land used for residential purposes. We generally do not realize how much is publicly owned, or how closely it is intermingled with private land in every part of each city.

The location of publicly owned areas (parks, especially), their improvements, and their connection to other publicly owned areas (streets, particularly) exert a powerful effect upon the use of privately owned land. The character of the streets, which enable rapid travel from suburb to central city, has often been a factor leading to suburban growth, for instance. Preferred residential areas have good parks and good schools, among other things. In numerous indirect ways, the use and improvement of the publicly owned land affects the kind of use of the intermingled private land.

The general public exercises a more direct influence over the use of individual privately owned tracts by the services it provides to them. Sewers, water supply, schools, and other group or social services are particularly important to small tracts of private land. Their provision often has encouraged people to move into new areas, where such services were made available. Some means exist to avoid the necessity for these group services—septic tanks instead of sewers, wells instead of city water supply, particularly. But these are frequently unsatisfactory substitutes, especially for intensive use of the private land. In some cases, people have

145

built houses on private land and then demanded provision of these public services, rather than waiting for them to be built first.

The general public exercises a still more direct control over private land use through zoning, subdivision control, and other regulatory measures. Such public laws or regulations tell people which uses are permitted and which are prohibited, on their own lands. By establishing the minimum size of lot, for instance, a subdivision regulation goes a long way toward determining the kind of a house to be built on the tract. Other regulations determine the distance by which buildings must be set back from the property line, and this in turn has often a major effect upon the land use. By these various means, the public narrows the range within which the private owner can exercise his own decision making and choice. The public action cannot be arbitrary or capricious; it must have a solid reason behind it. In the broadest terms, public control over use of private land in cities is based upon the dependence of the individual on the action of his neighbors, which we discussed earlier in this chapter. The general public, acting through government at some level, puts limits on private action in order to reduce the damage which some individuals may do to their neighbors. Some individual freedom is lost for the good of the group as a whole; one cannot open a beer parlor in the midst of a good residential neighborhood, to use an extreme example.

HOW URBAN LAND IS USED

The area of land per 100 residents runs as high as 30 acres for the average city of less than 5,000 total population; but then it gradually declines as the size of the city increases until it is 5 acres or less for cities of a quarter million or more inhabitants. This is simply another way of saying that the intensity of land use rises as the city size increases. The intensity of use rises for almost every use of the land. We have already noted that the area in streets and other public uses declines, relative to population, as the size of the city

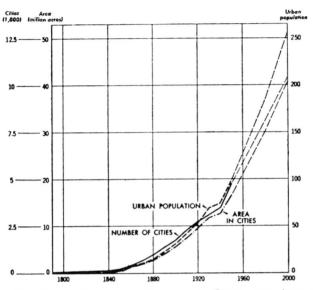

FIG. 28.—URBAN POPULATION, NUMBER OF CITIES, AND AREA OF CITIES IN THE UNITED STATES, 1790–1950, AND PROJECTIONS TO 2000

The number of cities, their area, and their population have increased at remarkably similar rates in the past, and promise to do so in the future. By the year 2000, each of these three measures will be at more than double its 1950 level. In the second half of the twentieth century, the problems of urban expansion may well be greater than they have been in all the past history of our country.

increases. The intensity of land use also rises in the average residential area of cities of various size. In small cities, with less than 10,000 total population, there are on the average about 12 to 14 people per acre of residential use;

147

in cities of a quarter million or more total population, this proportion rises to 50 or more people, on the average. More people live in apartments, and the apartment houses average larger in size, in the larger cities; more people also live in row houses, and even more in detached houses sitting on relatively small lots. There is even proportionately less gardening in the larger cities.

A similar relationship exists for industrial and commercial land uses, although the areas are not as large. As cities grow larger, the intensity of these uses rise, and their area per 100 total population is less. The same is true of land occupied by railroads. In recent years there has been some reversal of this relationship as the larger cities have developed suburbs, in which land use for commercial and industrial purposes tends to be spread over larger areas than in the older downtown districts. But even these sprawling suburbs sometimes use land more intensively than do the very small independent cities.

RACE, ECONOMIC CLASS, AND URBAN LAND USE

The older residential parts of every city deteriorate physically, as the buildings get old and outdated. What were once fine houses and apartments become less attractive as the years roll by, and many people who can afford to move to newer and better housing do so. Sometimes it is not the older folks who move, but their children, who establish their homes in other parts of the city. As the higher-income groups move out or are replaced, the housing comes to be used by successively lower-income groups. Often the older properties are not well maintained, and in order for the lower-income groups to afford this housing, they must crowd up much more than the structures were originally designed to accommodate. A cycle of deterioration sets in, which culminates in something everyone will recognize as a slum. This in time may be cleared by public action, and new structures built on the area. Later in this chapter we shall explore this process in a little more detail. But the new structures, even if residential, are of a very different type from the old ones. No obsolete residential part of any American city has ever yet been rebuilt by the same kind of housing as it had originally.

By this process, over the years residential areas tend to get sorted out according to the economic class and income of their occupants. Some areas are occupied by people of high annual incomes. It is not only that the cost of the house is high, and that its annual maintenance requires a relatively large amount of money, but the whole structure of life is different in such communities. Other communities are occupied by middle-income families, and still other areas by low-income families. The separation by income is not absolute; there is always some variation in income within each kind of community. The low-income groups often pay a higher percentage of their income for housing than do the higher-income classes, and often get less in terms of space and amenities for each dollar spent; but their low income often restricts their choice so drastically that they cannot do better.

This whole sorting out of urban residential areas by income classes is greatly complicated by racial considerations. The higher-income areas, especially the newer suburbs, have striven desperately by various means to keep Negroes out. Their measures have generally been effective —and often illegal. To a very large extent, the Negroes have been bottled up in the central cities, adding greatly to their overcrowding and to the deterioration nearly always consequent upon overcrowding. All major American cities now have a largely Negro core, with largely or wholly white suburbs. Because Negroes tend to have lower incomes than whites, they would in any case be largely concentrated in the older, less desirable residential centers of the larger cities; but the racial restrictions have greatly intensified this situation. Many Negro families that would be able to afford good suburban housing are unable to find a home outside of these centers; many more cannot afford to live elsewhere.

SLUMS

The end product of this whole process is slums, in the worst sense of the word. The older housing would in time become less attractive anyway, simply because of its age. But the occupation of some houses in such communities by lower-income groups, and the crowding that nearly always accompanies this occupation, makes the whole area less desirable to live in. Those who can afford to do so, and who are not barred by racial restrictions, tend to move elsewhere; they feel they cannot stem the tide of deterioration. Thus a vicious cycle is set up, a process which feeds upon itself. The usual end product of this process is a slum, of a most undesirable kind.

In the past thirty years or so, the nation has had a slum removal and urban renewal program. This program has certainly resulted in the removal of some of the worst such areas in many of the larger American cities. In spite of considerable public subsidy, the land values after clearing have been so high that the only kind of housing which seems economical is high-rise apartments, with high density of land use. In spite of every effort to keep costs to a minimum, including some subsidization, the resulting apartments are suitable only for middle-income families, not for families of the lowest income. The latter have been, in effect, pushed out of the old areas and forced to seek new areas, where they tend to hasten the deterioration of the latter. This has not only been a hardship on the displaced persons; it often has led to the charge that slum clearance has created as many new slums as it has removed old ones. The whole program has been subject to a great deal of criticism on these and other grounds.

More recently public programs have been undertaken to help people in the "gray" areas, those lying between the slums and the suburbs, maintain the physical condition and sociological character of their areas. This often involves measures for physical repair, modernization, and improvement of the properties; but it also involves a different attitude toward housing and living than has often prevailed in the past. Many of the people who live in such areas lack the financial resources to carry out these programs; more importantly, the will to do so and the leadership to organize people are also lacking. Because of the interrelationship between one family and another, to which we made reference earlier in this chapter, an individual family is sharply limited in what it can do alone. Maintenance of a neighborhood is peculiarly a group undertaking; unless there is group organization and group spirit, it probably cannot succeed. It is too soon yet to tell how well these new programs may work out.

Although slums have been attacked as evils in themselves, it is becoming increasingly clear that they are but one of the results of a basically worse and more fundamental problem, namely that of poor income distribution, or poverty. When total family income is low, not merely housing is bad; many other aspects of life are highly unsatisfactory also. Although our reference has been to housing, yet everyone knows that juvenile delinquency is high in slum areas, that there is much unemployment and illness there, and that in total life exhibits many undesirable aspects. Moreover, these problems tend to leave their imprint upon the children raised in such circumstances, and thus to a degree slums are self-perpetuating. This intimate and complex interrelationship raises a major policy question: should the public attack be directed primarily at slums, as evils in themselves, or should it be directed toward massive poverty itself? The latter is more difficult; the former seems more manageable, yet this may well be an illusion. Certainly this is a policy issue as yet unsettled, which shall assume greater importance in the future, and which will demand more thought and consideration than we have yet given it.

CHAPTER 15

Forest Land Ownership and Management

At several places in this book we have mentioned or discussed forests; now it seems desirable to consider forests a little more fully, especially as to their present ownership and condition, and also as to the problems that they now pose to us.

When colonization of what is now the United States first began, about half of the entire present area of the 48 contiguous states was forested. Most of the area east of the Mississippi River was covered with forest, only a little being open plains; a large part of the first tier of states west of that river was also forested, and in addition extensive areas in the Rocky Mountains and along the Pacific Coast.

Over the decades, the role of forests in American life has changed greatly. The forests furnished fuel and building material to the colonists, and in this respect they were a help to them, as we have already described in Chapter 3. But they had to be cleared before agriculture could be undertaken, and they long harbored the Indians who from time to time would attack the settlements; in these respects they were a serious problem for the colonists. As time went on, the obstacles gradually declined; the Indian menace was taken care of by military campaigns, and the land suitable for agriculture was gradually cleared. By the beginning of the twentieth century forests were valued chiefly as a source of building materials. Today we value the wood

153

that trees produce, for we can use it in many ways; we also value the watershed value of the forests, and their value for recreation. The colonists, and those who followed them for many decades, believed that the forests were "inexhaustible." They could travel for days on end through the forest, and its area and volume of trees indeed seemed

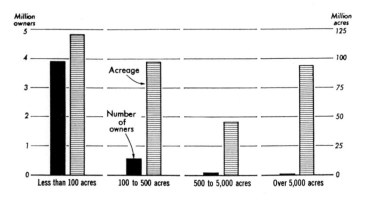

FIG. 29.—FOREST AREA, BY SIZE OF HOLDING

The distribution of forest land among owners of various sizes is even more extreme than is the distribution of farm output among farms of different sizes. A minuscule percentage of the largest forests contain a fourth of the whole acreage, but 4 million of the smallest forests contain less than half of the whole area. The latter have little prospect of profitable return because of their small size.

limitless. In fact, given the tools the colonists worked with, it was almost so. But this attitude remained long after the supply of mature timber had dwindled and while new growth was often slow in taking its place. Today we recognize that the forests have very definite limits, but at the same time we as a nation have undertaken many steps to make our forests more productive than formerly. Within the last decade or two, probably for the first time since white men began to cut forests seriously in this country, growth and drain (cut plus losses from fire, disease, and insects) are in balance.

Today the forests of the United States fall into five major groups, as far as ownership is concerned. First there are the federally owned forests; less than a fifth of the forested area, they contain more than two fifths of the volume of standing timber. Second are the publicly owned forests other than federal—those owned by states, counties, and other local government. They are much smaller, with about 5 per cent of the area and a slightly smaller proportion of the standing timber. Third, the forest industries own only slightly less area than the federal government, but these lands contain substantially less volume of standing timber. Fourth are the farm forests, the largest single ownership class, with about a third of the total area but less than half that percentage of the standing timber. Last there are private forests not owned by timber industries or in farms— the inevitable "other" classification. They are next largest in area to the farm forests, more than twice as large as the forest industry holdings, but they have a relatively low volume of timber.

In general, the federal forests are well managed, as we have described in Chapter 12, in spite of some rather serious deficiencies in the budget-appropriation processes of the federal government. The other publicly owned forests are similarly managed, but not quite as well on the whole.

Several factors tend to keep forestry from being highly profitable. It is true that a long period usually intervenes between the planting of a tree and its harvest—twenty years for southern pine grown for pulpwood, seventy-five to one hundred and twenty-five years for Douglas fir grown for lumber. But this factor alone would not necessarily be serious. A much more serious problem is the slow average growth rate of most trees; for the nation, forest lands add only about 5 per cent growth to the standing volume of timber each year. As soon as a tree is marketable at all, many a forest owner converts it into cash, which he can invest elsewhere at a higher return. To the forester this is poor forestry, because the tree is often cut just as it is entering its most productive growth period; but it may be good business to the forest owner pressed for cash. Risks of loss from fire, disease, and insects are further factors for immediate harvest. Also, forest investments are often not liquid, so that the owner may have difficulty getting his money out promptly if he needs it for something else. These are general obstacles or problems for forestry; some sizes and kinds of owners have still further problems, whereas others have found effective ways of coping with their problems.

LARGER PRIVATE FORESTS

Before entering into a discussion of the special features of the larger private forests, it is well to consider what we mean by "larger." On the average, forest land in the United States is one sixth as productive as crop land in farms. There is great variation within each, of course; but average farm land tends to produce more, and profitably to absorb more labor and capital, than does the average forest land. If one had a forestry enterprise, selling sawlogs or pulpwood, and wished to have a *minimum* efficient harvesting crew on a year-round basis, he would need from 10,000 to 20,000 acres in order to operate on a sustained yield basis. This is perhaps the absolute minimum unit, although an owner with less land, if he had some supplementary activity, might operate with limited profit. If one had an integrated operation, with only a minimum sawmill operation, a substantially larger acreage would be required. The exact area would vary according to the timber type and the kind of lumber making and manufacturing carried on. Many sawmills operate without owning any land, by buying timber wherever they can get it. There are substantial further economies in larger operations, if timber volumes are high enough to provide a good annual harvest near the processing plant. Since the Second World War, there has been a major trend toward merging already relatively large forestry manufacturing enterprises into much larger ones. An area of one quarter of a million acres to a million acres is not exceptionally large for a large modern forest products manufacturing plant.

In 1953 there were about 300 private forest owners with 50,000 or more acres of forest land each; their holdings averaged about 200,000 acres each. Most of these were forest industry firms—that is, firms that also had forest processing plants and whose main interest was forestry. But some fell in the "other" category discussed above. The latter group generally sold their logs to processors. On the whole, these forests are as well managed as are the federally owned forests. There were nearly 2,500 private forests of 5,000 to 50,000 acres, averaging about 14,000 acres each. On the basis of earlier calculations, these are just about minimum efficiency units for timber harvest but not for timber processing. These forests are, on the average, fairly well managed, but not as well as the larger ones.

The larger private forests are scattered throughout the forested parts of the nation. They are especially common on the Pacific Coast, where forestry operations tend to be relatively large; some are found in the South, especially by companies making pulp and paper; and a few are found elsewhere. Some large forest owners operate in more than one region. In general the forests included in these larger holdings are naturally productive forests, and their present productivity is relatively high. While there is considerable variation among them, on the whole they offer a reasonable prospect for profitable forestry operation. Part of their area is poorly stocked, perhaps to poor species, part needs re-planting, and there are other deficiencies. But on the whole the prospects for future maintenance of these forests is good.

These larger forest owners have generally shown considerable sensitivity to the public demands for recreational use of their forests. Most owners permit hunting and fishing on their land, and many maintain campgrounds or other facilities, sometimes available only on payment of a fee but often available free. One can indeed wonder why the public should feel that it has a right to use these lands; the owners certainly undergo some expense and bother in making the land available for public use, and the use is surely a valuable privilege. For public relations reasons, many larger forest landowners would hesitate to impose a use charge; yet fairness would seem to indicate that the public should be required to pay a reasonable fee.

The larger forest owners enjoy special federal tax relief. Production of forest products pays only a capital gains tax of 25 per cent, rather than a corporation tax of 52 per cent or a personal income tax that might well run over 40 per cent for persons of large income. While this income tax relief is available to all forest owners, in practice it is meaningful only to those owners who would otherwise have to pay a higher personal rate—namely, the larger owners. This tax advantage is particularly valuable to the largest forest owners; without it, their forestry operations would often be much less profitable.

SMALL PRIVATE FORESTS

The large number and small average size of the "small" privately owned forests in the United States almost stagger the imagination. In this connection, our earlier comments as to the meaning of "small" must be recalled. Forest land is, on the average, about one sixth as productive as farm land. Hence, 1,800 acres of forest land is about as productive as 300 acres of farm land—and the average farm in the United States has 300 acres of land. Many farms, however, are substandard economic units. As we have noted, from 10,000 to 20,000 acres of land is needed for a minimum economic forestry unit, on a sustained yield basis.

There are about 46,000 privately owned forests of 500 to 5,000 acres each; they contain about 10 per cent of all commercial forestry land in the United States. Their net productivity rating is very much lower than that of the forest industry and federal forests. About half of these forests are parts of farms, most of the rest fall in the miscellaneous or "other" land ownership classification. By the standards listed above, these are far from economic units, if operated alone; in combination with some other business activity, some of them may produce some significant income.

There are more than ten times as many forests of 100 to 500 acres, and they contain twice as much land, as the former group; and their net productivity ratings are even lower. And below this are nearly 4 million forests of less than 100 acres, containing still more land, with a still lower net productivity rating! These are truly the infants, yet there are so many of them that their total area is considerable.

Many of these small privately owned forests had inherently low productivity even when covered with virgin timber. Because of poor soil, poor climate, steep slopes, or for other reasons their rate of growth was always low. Most of them have been cut, usually several times, generally in an exploitative manner, and today they typically have a small volume of low-quality growing stock. These forests could be rehabilitated and made more productive. Seedlings should be set out where needed, trees of poor form or low-value species should be cut to allow the better ones to grow, and other measures could be taken. These various measures would cost some immediate outlay; more seriously, many years would often be required before substantial volumes could be harvested. Though the physical possibilities for greatly increased output exist, the economic possibilities are meager. The economic possibilities of private forests can be summarized as in Figure 30.

Size of forest tract (acres)	Total acreage in this size class (millions of acres)	Economic prospects for good forestry (based on size alone)
Over 50,000	58	Good to excellent
5,000 to 50,000	35	Good
500 to 5,000	46	Fair to good; most such units are below optimum size to form an economic forest unit by themselves; most require some specialized management in addition to the owners; but some economic incentives to good forestry do exist on the larger tracts of better site quality.
100 to 500	98	Fair; such forests are often sidelines to some other economic activity; larger farm forests, if well stocked, may offer a fair prospect; poorer and smaller farm forests offer very little economic incentive; among "other" forests, the better ones offer some prospects if under some form of group or supervised management
Under 100	121	Poor to nonexistent, except in case of farm forests integrated with agricultural enterprise, or unless combined with other ownerships for management purposes.

FIG. 30.—ECONOMIC POSSIBILITIES OF PRIVATE FORESTS

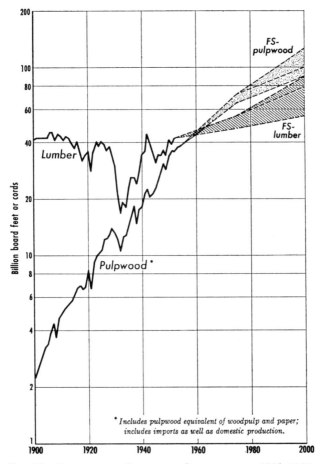

FIG. 31.—LUMBER AND PULPWOOD CONSUMPTION, 1900–1955,
AND ALTERNATIVE PROJECTIONS, 1975 AND 2000

Lumber is one major raw material whose consumption has not risen
as national population and income have increased over the past fifty
years; it has gradually been replaced by other construction materials.
Paper, on the other hand, is an increasingly necessary part of our
complex modern economy and society.

With the economic prospects for so much of this land so poor, it is fairly obvious that many persons own such land for nonpecuniary reasons. In a good many instances, the "forest" is some woodland which is part of a farm; the farm owner may not really wish to own and operate forest land, but cannot very well get rid of it on any profitable or rational operating basis. Many such small forests are owned for recreation purposes, or out of sentiment because the land has long been in the family, or in hope of speculative gain in value, or as a hedge against inflation, or for some other reason not connected at all with the productivity of the forest. Many such owners are under serious illusion as to the true worth of their land for these other purposes; the speculative gains are seldom realized, for instance. But it is clear that most such owners are unwilling or unable to provide good forest management to such small properties. Moreover, in most cases the financial returns from very much better forestry simply would not pay the costs involved, especially if the necessary labor and supervision must be hired.

A NATIONAL POLICY FOR SMALL PRIVATE FORESTS

Does the nation really need the increased output of forest products which a higher level of management of these small private forests could call forth? The United States Forest Service, after its study of future needs for forest products, has concluded that the output of these small forests must be stepped up; some other private analysts have agreed with it, but the forest industry, by and large, does not feel that a stepped-up output from these lands will be seriously needed in the future.

If we should conclude that the present low level of output must be stepped up, how should we go about increasing it? In the past the answer has been education directed at these small forest owners. This was on the assumption that the major reason that farm and other small forest owners did not practice good forestry was because they did not know how to do so. Past educational efforts have reached only a very small fraction of the small private forest landowners, and seem not to have been effective with them. If economic gains of good forestry have been less than the costs, then forest owners have been wise from their own standpoint not to engage in the kind of forestry recommended to them by forestry experts. The difficulty has been more deep-seated than merely lack of knowledge.

Another public program in the past, available to small and large private forest owners alike, has been cooperative forest fire prevention and control. Federal funds have been available to the states, some of the latter have supplemented these funds, and private owners have made varying amounts of cooperative effort. A whole community gains from effective fire control; burned-over forest areas injure the whole community, by their very unsightliness if by nothing else. As a result of intensive fire prevention and control programs extending over many years, the damage to forests from fire today is less than the damage from insects and disease.

Some other programs have been available to small private forest owners. In a few cases technical help in actual forestry operations has been available. Seedlings for planting have been available, either free or at nominal cost. These types of programs have been provided by forest industry firms in some cases, as well as by public agencies. However, in total they have reached only a small fraction of the very large number of small private forest owners.

If the full physical potential of these small forests is to be achieved, public programs on a vastly bigger scale than any in the past are necessary. But what kind of public programs, if any, would really be effective? Various kinds of subsidies, grants, aids, and incentives might be offered, of course; but could they fulfill their purpose? To do so, they would have to reach a major portion of the literally millions of small owners; this would be difficult at best. A substantial incentive would be necessary to make it worthwhile for many small forest owners to improve their operations significantly; and this might be a quite costly program in relation to the results.

If any kind of special program were undertaken, it seems clear that it should differentiate among small forest owners according to the size of their holding, and according to the site quality or inherent productivity of their land. Among the small owners, the prospects for good forestry are better, the larger is the forest holding and the better is the site.

CHAPTER 16

A Look Back—And Ahead

This book has sought to give a rather brief and general history of white—and black—man on the land of the United States. It is not history in the sense of legislation passed, elections won or lost, wars waged, or specific dates. It has been concerned rather with what man did on the land. As such, it has dealt particularly with the relation of man to man in the use of land. The technical side of land use is important, but the social or institutional side is often more so. To fit into the space available in a short book, the discussion has necessarily had to be in general terms; a myriad of further details exists on every point. Other writers might have chosen a different emphasis upon the details of this history, but most scholars, I think, would agree as to the broad outlines of the story we have pictured here. It has not been our purpose to advance new and novel theses but rather to put the accepted facts into proper perspective and sequence.

We have emphasized the importance of the colonial period in American land history. Even the antecedents of that colonialism were significant. By modern standards the colonial society and economy were small indeed. Yet it was at this period that the seeds were planted which today have grown into our whole land use and tenure system. The colonial period was followed by the early national period; a major problem in the new nation was the use of its newly acquired public domain. For many decades the most single

165

important aspect of national government was the management of the public domain. At first, and for a long time, disposal was dominant—wholesale, heedless, even reckless disposal which saw about two thirds of the public domain, acquired by purchase and treaty, pass out of federal ownership. But the very speed and recklessness of that disposal led to demand for retention of some lands in public ownership. This formed the basis of a large federal estate, which has gone through different stages of management. The problems of land use and land tenure today are no less important than they ever were, but a vast complex of other national and of international problems today clamors for the attention of the President and the Congress, until land matters receive relatively little attention.

We have examined briefly land tenure and land use in Latin America; our system and theirs are in sharp contrast in many ways. By and large we are fairly well satisfied with the total land situation in our country. Many Latin Americans are deeply dissatisfied with the situation in their respective countries; the threat of uprising and revolution is present in many countries. To us, typical Latin American methods of land tenure and land use seem seriously deficient. If we have reason for satisfaction with our situation, let us thank our remote ancestors, not lay claim to great virtue in ourselves! The seeds of the land tenure and land use practices in this country and in Latin America were laid in their respective colonial periods.

We have also looked at the various major land uses in the United States today; we have tried to describe the major problems of the city, the farm, and the forest. All of this historical treatment brings us down to the present. Hopefully, it helps us to understand where we now are, as well as how we got here. To this author, this history is dramatic and significant. He can only hope that he has communicated some of the drama and importance to the reader.

Where do we go from here? It is typical of the modern world to be concerned with the future. The tendency is perhaps more marked in the United States than in some countries, but it is more a modern than an old-fashioned attitude. We expect the population and the total economy to grow bigger, and we want and expect to have our way of living grow better also; we are generally optimistic about the future. People have not always looked at the future thus. Many societies have really lived in the past, venerating everything that was old, merely tolerating the present, and scarcely ever looking ahead. When they did look ahead, it was more often than not in pessimistic terms, perhaps forecasting doom and disaster. When we look ahead optimistically, however, it need not be blindly—we can see problems and yet be confident of our ability to solve them.

In the last few pages of this book, I shall not try to forecast the future. Rather I will raise some policy issues and pose some problems—issues and problems which must be faced in some way in the decades ahead. There are no easy answers to these or to any problems that are worthy of serious consideration. You younger readers will face some kind of land problems all your lives; if you manage to solve the problems which I pose, then you can be sure others will rise to demand an answer. Let us raise these problems around different kinds of present land use.

Urban land.—What kind of a city do we want to live in? Every present trend points in the direction of a nation of city dwellers, but the kind of city is ours to choose and to make. Shall we continue to grow in continuously sprawling suburbs, with many people living farther and farther from downtown, with the city center largely decayed, the home of Negroes and other disadvantaged groups, and with the suburbs lily white? One can look at trends of the past few years and estimate from them that this is what we shall have. Or can we somehow reduce the sharply class-structured nature of our cities, so that each part of the city is more nearly a cross-section of the whole? Can we somehow rehabilitate the parts of the city nearer into the center? In the growing areas, can we cluster settlement, so as to have larger blocks of open space intermingled where people live? Can we reduce the pollution of air and water which cities usually cause? All in all, can we make the city a pleasanter place in which to live, although much larger than on the average today, and can we facilitate better contact with nature? These are some of the larger questions; many more detailed ones could be added. Each of them involves land use and land tenure aspects, although each also involves other aspects. They are peculiarly group problems; the individual, no matter how hard he tries, cannot solve many of them alone.

Land for parks, recreation, and open space.—What kind of outdoor activities do we want? Where? And how much land and water do we need? Given a multiplicity of public agencies at the federal, state, and local levels of government, and given a number of private groups, all interested in parks and open space, how can we get better coordinated planning than we have had in the past? By what means can we best pay for the extensive areas that will almost certainly be needed in the future—by general taxes, by special taxes, by charges to be paid by park users, or by some combination of these and perhaps other means? Can we find ways in which we can persuade private landowners to make their land available for general public recreational use, perhaps on payment of modest fees? While the individual may have an attractive yard around his house, most park and outdoor recreation areas will be either public or developed for considerable numbers of people. Like that of the development of urban land, the provision of parks and recreation areas is mostly a group problem.

Land for agriculture.—Agriculture is saddled with twin problems today: poverty and surplus. A substantial proportion of all farmers have very low incomes, in large part because their land area and other productive resources are so poor. How can the nation shrink back its labor force in agriculture to the number actually needed? How can we help older farmers attain better living conditions, or ease for them the pain of readjustments? In many rural communities, where young men are shunning small farms that promise nothing but unrewarding toil and hardship, preferring instead to move to the cities, how can we help a smaller number of able young farmers develop many fewer but much larger and more efficient farms, in order to perpetuate sounder rural communities? The commercial part of agriculture, by its very efficiency, has produced a burdensome surplus of several crops. Both the demand and the supply of such crops are highly inflexible, and sharply fluctuating prices or government controls seem to have been the only alternatives until now. Can we develop a better and less expensive solution to the problems of this segment of agriculture? Although we have been plagued by surpluses, are we sure that we have adequate reserves and sufficient flexibility to cope with national disaster?

Forest land.—How great is the distant national need for forest products? Many, if not most, measures effective for increasing the supply of forest products in the distant future must be undertaken soon, if they are to be effective when needed. This is why present forecasts of future demand for forest products are so important. How can the nation get the most from the public and large forest industry forests—especially recreation and other values in addition to logs? What shall we do with the vast number of very small and unproductive small private forests? Is there some way in which their output can be economically increased? Shall we as a nation undertake a "crash" program

169

for these forests, along lines not now very clear, or shall we simply let them drift, producing what nature unaided can produce? These are the major policy questions facing the country as far as forest lands are concerned.

Land for highways.—How can we make the highways of the whole country serve us better? They are built to move goods and people, and to make possible uses of land that otherwise could not be possible. But is this enough? Might not travel along the highways be made more enjoyable and mentally more stimulating, as well as physically comfortable and speedy? Is "pretty" scenery along the highway enough, or might we gain some idea of the natural resources, the history, and the culture of the countryside through which we are driving? Should highways be located primarily to serve presently existing traffic, or should they also be planned to direct land use and economic development along desired lines?

One could draw up a longer and more detailed list of land policy issues, but these seem to be the main ones, of nation-wide scope and importance. They nearly all demand public action of some kind, and public action means public decisions.

170

Index

171

173

174